KEEPING IT REAL

Keeping it real

Lessons I've Learned as A Real Estate Agent

Chris Phillips

Copyright © 2020 Chris Phillips

All Rights Reserved.

ISBN: 9798615146732

No portion of this book may be reproduced in any form without permission from the publisher, except as permitted by U.S. Copyright law.

R.H.P

DEDICATION

To the anonymous professionals everywhere who prove every day that honesty, quality, and respect are the virtues that matter most; And, by so doing, demonstrate the merits of humanity in the process.

TABLE OF CONTENTS

INTRODUCTION — i

1 DARWIN AND YOU — 19

2 CONSIDER THE HAND THAT FEEDS YOU — 35

3 SYMBOLS OF HUMANITY — 57

4 BEING A SALESPERSON — 71

5 THE LAW OF OPPORTUNITY — 85

6 SCREW THE GURU — 105

7 THE THREE WHY'S — 123

8 THE RIGHT BUSINESS FOR ME? — 139

9 EKG INCOME — 151

10 ASSUMPTIONS AND EXPECTATIONS — 163

11 BEWARE OF MOTIVATION — 177

12 HOMES ARE EMOTIONAL THINGS — 189

13 THE TOBACCO OF TIME — 205

14 FORGET TO BE AFRAID — 223

15 THE NEW RULES OF REAL ESTATE — 237

introduction

I wrote this book for three distinct reasons.

The first is because **the Real Estate industry, and the income potential found therein, has changed my life forever.** This book is my humble attempt to give back to the business that has given me so much.

This profession has allowed me to provide for my family in ways that I would never have imagined possible. It's been a crazy ride, but one for which I'll always be grateful. Embarking as an agent was a significant personal risk, but that leap of faith is something I'll never regret as long as I live.

However, for all of the success and perspective this career has given me, it's also been one of the most mentally and emotionally difficult things I've ever done; and I suspect the same for you, regardless of how long you've been in the business.

Contrary to what many people think, being a Real Estate agent—a good Real Estate agent—is hard-ass work.

No matter how the shows on HGTV make it seem, success in the Real Estate game is anything but guaranteed and is far from glamorous. It often feels like walking a financial tightrope with no net below to catch you if you fall. That feeling of precariousness is especially true for those who are just starting out.

I've been there—believe you me.

That brings me to the second reason I wrote this book:

The Real Estate game is an emotional game.

It's emotional for clients and it's emotional for agents.

In a world where transactions and professional interaction are occurring in an increasingly digital space, Real Estate is an industry where two emotional creatures—called "people"—still get together around a kitchen table to work towards accomplishing a common goal.

What this implies is that Real Estate deals don't happen in an emotional vacuum or on a sterile spreadsheet, regardless of how much we may want them to. Transactions are full of nuance, nerves, and narcissism because of the human beings that bring that baggage to every kitchen table. It's part of who we are. We (agents and clients) are messy, emotional headcases who have hopes, dreams, fears, doubts, insecurities, and anxieties about living this thing called "life."

To that point, instead of a book with sales scripts or conversation manipulation techniques, I wanted to contribute something a little more thoughtful.

I'm going to address the anxieties agents feel and the emotions that drive clients and their erratic behavior. I'm going to explore fear and how it affects agents and clients alike, often at the same time, without the other side realizing it.

I'm also going to call out some of the bullshit traditions we have in our "professional" culture. Make no mistake, there's valid reasons why Real Estate agents are consistently ranked as some of the least trustworthy professionals out there. There's a nasty underbelly to our profession, and we need to start talking about it

—I'm looking at you, Guru Brokers.

Finally, **the over-arching reason I wrote this book is to help you, in a genuine and sincere way.**

And, maybe "help" is the wrong term.
I won't try to teach, or lecture, or pontificate some "secret knowledge" that I have that you don't. There are plenty of others out there who are willing to do that—and charge you $899 per month in the name of "coaching."

No, more than anything, my intent is to let you know that you're not alone, whatever problem you're facing.

I know what it's like to leave Corporate America because you hate every literal minute of every damn day of cubicle life. I can share a few thoughts with you on the subject of being an excited, young licensee who finds reality much more difficult than the Real Estate books promised. I empathize with the young parents who have mortgage payments, maxed out credit cards, and empty deal pipelines.

I'm not sure if you've noticed, but Real Estate agents LOVE to pretend like everything is fine, and that all is well with their business, while their deal just fell through and they're freaking out.

Yes, we agents are great at pretending like we've got our shit together when we're at the seminar in Las Vegas while, in the back of our mind, we're not sure if we can make the payment on the car lease we got to appear like a badass.

As terrifying as those times of uncertainty are, it's the lessons learned in those harrowing moments—when you face the very real possibility of professional death—that you learn the very principals needed to not only survive, but succeed.

The approach I've taken when writing is to picture you and I sitting down for lunch together—to speak to you as if I'm speaking to a friend.

I'll be honest and open about the challenges facing modern agents. I'll also be candid and direct about the nuances of service and emotional intelligence that will set you apart in the modern marketplace.

At the end of the day, people are what make this business move. Relationships are the paramount principal of success. Looking at people, understanding them, and then serving them as honestly as you can, is the single most important "idea" I can offer.

There's no script that replaces service; no talk that replaces trust.

Serve people well and you'll never need to learn another script again. That's my advice to you in your dealings with clients, and it's the philosophy I've used as I've written this book.

Let's get to it.

Chris

chapter one

Darwin and You

"It is not the most intellectual of the species that survives; the species that survives is the one that is able to adapt to and to adjust best to the changing environment in which it finds itself."
- Charles Darwin

Nobody wants to admit it, but the Real Estate game is changing.

The Monopoly man has packed up his monocle and retired to Florida; Park Place is listed for sale on Redfin.

Like the massive meteorite that struck Earth 65 million years ago, the internet recently slammed into the surface of the home buying marketplace causing a plume of dust, debris, and radioactive fallout.

Home buyers and sellers are shifting their attitudes and behaviors en mass when it comes to how they buy and sell homes.

However, if you ask around, it seems there are those in the industry who deny this change is taking place. Like "flat earthers" living on a round globe, they proclaim that "everything is fine, we've seen this before."

They're wrong.

Ignoring the elephant in the room, agents, brokers, and lenders are still sipping champagne in their finest clothes as the walls burn down around them. They're either unable or unwilling to see more than 5 feet in front of them, failing to distinguish the impact smoke from their cigar smoke. Some of these legacy professionals—those who've been in the industry a while—probably do see the changes, but simply don't care; they've long since made their money. To them, the future of the industry is irrelevant because their bank account is sufficiently padded.

But, unlike the fat and happy brokers of yesteryear, *you* don't have the luxury of ignoring your current market reality; and we, as an industry, damn well better stop taking lessons from those whose heads are in the sand.

A shift is required for the industry at large. A generational event has taken place, and we're required to adapt and evolve to stay relevant—to survive.

Despite all this, let me reassure you that the sky is not falling. While a massive, monumental shift has—and is—occurring, it does not mean life is over, or that we must pack up our faux leather briefcases and head home.

This market shift, like a wildfire sparked by lightning, will *not* hopelessly result in carnage, industry death, or simmering bits of Realtor charcoal. No, this change—this techno-philosophical shift in how the world buys property—presents a tremendous *opportunity* for those who see it. Like the new growth that sprouts through fallen ash, if you're wise enough to read the writing on the burning walls, you'll see significant economic prosperity on the other side.

Thriving times are yet ahead for those with vision, for those who are willing to work to make it real.

But, make no mistake, the rules have changed.

And so, must you.

Phenotypic Real Estate

In case you're unfamiliar with Darwin's theory of evolution, let me give you a summary. And don't freak out over the "science words." Take a deep breath and trust me. This will help you see the Real Estate industry differently than 95% of the agents out there.

In Darwin's theory, there is a term used to describe certain attributes of living things, called *phenotype*. Phenotypes are basically a set of genetic characteristics that influence how a person or animal interacts with their environment. Examples of phenotypes include the shape of a bird's beak, the length of a fox's tail, or the size of a person's foot.

Every living thing has a slightly different phenotype (genetic characteristics) than the other similar living things around it. Line up 10 birds of the same species and each one of them will have a beak ever so slightly unique to them because each bird has its own genetic code—like a fingerprint. All humans are human, but some are tall, and some are short. Some people have light hair and freckles, some have black hair and rich skin tones, etc.

Same species, slightly different physical traits.

The clincher is these physical characteristics, born from the slight genetic variations in our DNA, *change how we interact with our environment*, especially as genes are passed down from parent to child over multiple generations. Eventually, the result is a population of living things whose physical characteristics begin to *resemble the environment* in which they find themselves.

The classic example of this were small birds which Charles Darwin, the father of evolution, observed to be of the *same species*, yet had *different sizes and shapes* in their beaks. These slight beak differences allowed them to access the various kinds of food in their differing environments. Over the generations, birds with beak shape "A" ate "A" type food in "A" type environments. Birds with beak shape "B" who lived in "A" type environments didn't last long, because their beaks wouldn't allow them to eat as much, so they failed to reproduce, and died. The birds which did eat—and reproduce—were those whose beaks best matched their environment. Their offspring inherited beaks best suited to the food source around them. These little birds became known as "Darwin's Finches"

—and they have everything to do with your success in Real Estate.

Darwin's Finches

Make no mistake, our environment has changed. And our economic food source is now different than it was before.

This food source, rather than nuts or seeds, *is the economic behavior of the customer-clients around us.*

The good news for you, little Realtor finch, is that you have one advantage that Darwin's finches never had: the ability to change the shape of your beak—without having to die to do it.

Relics of History and Realities of Present

Real Estate, as an industry, has been around since the year 1900 (roughly) when brokers in Chicago, Baltimore, and St. Louis approached homeowners and offered to assist them in finding buyers for their property. For approximately the past 120 years, agents, and the industry they formed, cultivated the pattern of buying and selling property.

Over those many decades, as with many other budding professions, certain stereotypes were formed in the eyes of the general public. Like mechanics in overalls holding wrenches, or physicians in white coats with stethoscopes around their necks, Realtors came to have a certain image, or visual symbol, assigned to them.

I'm sure you're familiar with it:

Men and women in suits, carrying clipboards, smiling in the front yard of a Victorian home, as they dangle the keys over the cupped hands of a newlywed couple, whose arms are wrapped around each other's waists.

Large, red "SOLD" signs, along with golden retrievers and picket fences, are also standard issue accessories in these types of images.

In a historical sense, Real Estate agents came to be the professional gatekeepers of the American Dream. They were the symbol of home ownership. That image of keys being exchanged in the front yard became a rite of passage for generations of Americans as they approached the age of early adulthood; this was, of course, followed up by the ceremonial husband-carries-wife-through-the-front-door ritual, which basically certified the whole deal.

As you might have guessed by my continued use of the past tense, these symbols, images, and rituals aren't so commonplace anymore.

Turn on a football game this weekend and wait for a commercial break. It won't be long before an ad pops up advertising something home-ownership related, such as mortgages, home buying help, or home improvement. Next time one of these commercials comes on, I want you to count the number of times you see a Real Estate agent represented on screen.

The correct answer is: 0.

You will see zero representations of Realtors on screen, in advertisements, or attached to the concept of homes in general, in mainstream media.

Zilch. Zero. Nothing. Nada.

What will you see?

Apps. Scrolling websites. And, a few more apps.

You'll see ads for home automation, pushing buttons to get mortgages, and augmented reality living rooms where you can see what a couch looks like in your front room before you ever go to the store.

In short, you'll see lots and lots of *technology*.

You will see literally zero Real Estate agents.

Rest in Peace, stock photo golden retriever. You had a good run.

What does this lack of media acknowledgment mean for you as an agent? It means that symbols and stereotypes—our environments—are changing.

The Real Estate industry is evolving. Perceptions drilled into our minds by the relentless repetition—and deep pockets—of modern mega-advertisers, are shifting *away* from Realtors holding keys, and *towards* pushing virtual buttons on smartphones.

It means consumer behavior is changing.

Those consumers—those "seeds"—have different assumptions than they once did. When someone decides they need to sell their home and move, a Real Estate agent is no longer the first image to pop into their head. Due in mixed proportion to the omnipresence of the internet, incessant mass marketing, and our technological habits overall, people no longer jump right to agents as the solution to their Real Estate problems.

Sorry to break it to you Barbra, but if you've got a beak built for 1992, you don't have a shot in hell at cracking the "seeds" of modern millennials—or the increasingly tech-savvy boomer generation, for that matter.

The Forgotten Truths of Natural Selection

Now, with all this talk of meteors, market change, and fallen golden retrievers, I wouldn't be surprised if you're feeling a little down right now. You bought this book looking to succeed in your Real Estate business, and it may seem like I just took a giant shit on the entire industry. If that's indeed how you're feeling, let's lighten the mood by addressing the bright side:

Whenever people talk about evolution, they always focus on what changes, and rightly so. But, when we talk about adaptation, and "survival of the fittest," the one thing we seem to forget is the one thing I'm asking you to focus all of your professional attention on:

The things that stay the same—despite all the change.

From an evolutionary perspective, the things that stay the same—the things that remain behind after the chaos of change has burned away the weaknesses—are the strengths. The good news for the finch is that the finch doesn't need to become an eagle to survive. It needs only to remain a finch, just with a slightly different beak. The feathers, claws, eyes, and wings all get to stay because they're important. They're important because they work. They work because they're fundamental to the nature of the environment.

The Real Estate industry (our environment), and the agents who work in it (the finches), will not die; but they must adapt. Adaptation doesn't mean getting rid of everything we've ever done, it just means focusing more on the things that matter and casting away the things that don't.

In this business, the thing that matters most is the people for whom we work.

In a modern world full of sterile technology and supplanted personal relationships, the one thing we always seem to forget is that the phones that run those apps are still held by human hands. Those hands belong to a person, and it's that person who, despite themselves, has real problems that can only be solved by another real person—you. We can build websites and develop apps all day long, but it's people on both sides of the handshake that make this engine go.

Becoming increasingly focused—perhaps even a little obsessed—with the wants and needs of people, is the simple formula for changing the shape of your beak to meet the requirements of your new environment.

People are our environment. Focusing on them is how we come to resemble it.

In Real Estate, after all the change, the thing that remains the same is that people make the entire thing work. Houses are fundamental to the nature of people; People, therefore, are fundamental to the nature of houses.

Our job, as agents, is to understand the relationship between people and houses, and foster it in a way which preserves—and strengthens—our role as the stewards of home ownership in America. After all, we call ourselves "experts" don't we? Well, becoming a true expert, and providing the value that comes as a result, is a whole lot more difficult than just passing a test, or getting a license.

It requires something no app will ever offer: humanity.

You must change the shape of your beak by relentlessly focusing on your pre-existing phenotype of being a living, breathing human being who cares. Your ability to communicate to, empathize with, and understand the needs of, the people around you represents a different, yet still similar, "environment" which demands your unique phenotype of being human. People, and their thoughts, emotions, and problems, out of necessity, have now become your number one priority.

And that's the way it should be, because taking on other's problems as your own is exactly what they're paying you for, in case you forgot. Empathy, mixed with the ability to solve real problems, is what being a good agent is all about.

Not long ago, all someone needed to do to earn a living as an agent was pass a test, get access to the MLS, and join a brokerage. There were so many homes to buy and sell, and so few consumer options for how to do it, agents cornered the market in a true monopoly. Back then, you had only to find someone who wanted to buy/sell a home and get them to sign a contract.

Today, you must (1) find someone who wants to buy/sell, (2) convince them to work with an agent, and (3) they must *see value* in the service you provide because there are a dozen discount brokerages online willing to do it for next to nothing.

Like it or not, today's Real Estate reality requires more from all of us. Your job, and the new rule of Real Estate, is to focus on the only two people who ever closed a successful deal:

You—

—And the person for whom you work.

That, my fellow finch friend, will make all the difference in determining your survival, and success, in the years to come.

chapter two

CONSIDER THE HAND THAT FEEDS YOU

"Value is not determined by those who set the price. Value is determined by those who choose to pay it."
-Simon Sinek

The number one psychological mistake Real Estate agents make, is not asking this question:

"Why is my client paying me?"

Take a minute and think about that question under the two most common scenarios in our industry. I want you to answer this question, in your own mind, first, as if you were a listing agent, and then as if you were a buyer's agent.

Scenario A: Listing Agent

If you're sitting at the kitchen table of a homeowner whose door you just knocked on, and you're asking them to sign a listing agreement that states they owe you 6% of the proceeds of the sale of their home, what is it you're telling them you'll provide to justify that cost?

Think of it as a two-sided scale. On one side, you have the 6% fee; on the other side, you have your list of what you'll do for them.

Now if you're like most agents, your list probably includes these items:

- I'll list your house on the MLS
- I'll take photos of your house
- I'll "market" your house on my website
- I'll make flyers for you
- I'll knock on doors of your neighbors with those flyers
- I'll post your listing at my brokerage
- I'll put a sign in your front yard
- I'll schedule showings for you
- I'll give you tips on how to clean up your house
- I'll help you understand which offer is best

If your list looks something like this one, the internet will take your job from you, if it hasn't already.

In the eyes of the modern homeowner, that list of "services" is pathetic and isn't worth 1%—let alone 6%—of the value of that person's home.

In the Real Estate world we live in, you've got to give value for value or you will make a quick exit from the business.

Let's quickly break down just a couple of key problems with that typical list of "services."

Listing Proposition #1: "I'll List Your House on the MLS"

The MLS is nothing more than an online marketplace of homes being bought and sold in a certain geographical area. The news flash here is that homeowners no longer need you if they simply want their home listed on the MLS. There are plenty of internet brokers who will do that for them for a few hundred bucks. This is no longer a unique value proposition for modern agents. If you communicate to this homeowner that your #1 "service" is simply uploading a few photos and square footage numbers to a website, then you're overselling a poor service and underselling yourself.

Listing Proposition #2: "I'll Put A Sign in Your Front Yard"

Let's be real: the vast majority of home sales are not generated by 'For Sale' signs pounded into the front yard. That sign is just about as effective at generating sales as the inflatable stick man with flapping arms at the used car dealership. If you don't already know, the *actual* reason agents put those signs up is to generate buyer leads from the Lookie Loo's who call when they drive by on Sunday afternoons.

At best physical signs are an emotional rite of passage for the person selling the home; at worst, they're a disingenuous attempt to generate shitty buyer leads by the listing agent. They do almost nothing to actually get the home sold—and even if they did—a homeowner could put up their own damn sign. Again, not a valid justification for 6% of a home's value.

Listing Proposition #3: "I'll Give You Tips for Preparing Your Home"

Sorry to break it to you sweetheart, but you're not Joanna Gaines, nor will you ever be.

You're not an interior designer or an external landscaper. You don't understand feng shui and the homeowner already knows they should probably add a fresh coat of paint to the bedroom. They don't need you to tell them to mow the lawn or take the family photos off the wall. They have HGTV and Google. Aside from that, if this hypothetical client is really so stupid they need you to tell them to vacuum the carpet and throw out the trash before a showing, then they're not someone you want to waste your time with anyway. Pointing out the obvious need for new paint and tidiness is no reason to ask for a 6% commission.

Scenario B: Buyer's Agent

Now, let's look at the list of some common reasons Buyer's Agents use to justify their services:

- I have access to the key boxes
- I have access to homes for sale on the MLS
- I can send you "Hot Sheets" (i.e., new listing reports)
- I'm available to see houses on evenings and weekends
- I have access to "pocket listings" in my brokerage
- I work with lots of investors
- I can help you write the offer
- I'm good at spotting the "lemon" houses
- Your mom's coworker's vet's cousin's friend used me
- Don't worry, the seller pays my commission

Again, if you think any of these are valid reasons for someone to do business with you, then start preparing your resume, because you ain't gonna last long.

Buyer Proposition #1: "I Have MLS/Key Box Access"

I've said it once, I'll say it a hundred more times: MLS access is not adequate justification for why someone should work with you, to say otherwise is to suggest you're nothing more than a needless gatekeeper. The same goes for key box access.

Printing out MLS sheets, or popping open key boxes, proves nothing more than the fact that you passed a test and pay $40 per month to have a special app on your phone. It's not unique and it's not valuable. It certainly shouldn't be used as a relevant reason for someone to trust you with the process of making the largest financial transaction of their life.

Buyer Proposition #2: "Someone You Know Used Me"

This is a tricky one. I don't mean to suggest there isn't value in being referred by a past client, friend, or family member. Personal and professional referrals are the lifeblood of a strong business. The problem here is when we *assume* that someone should work with us *because* of a relationship. Simply "knowing" someone is not a valid economic reason for them to enlist your professional services. I can't tell you how often I've heard agents bitch and moan about the fact their friend or family member didn't "use" them to buy a house, as if the fact that they share common pieces of DNA somehow makes them a good agent.

Relationships and networks are great ways to start conversations or get your foot in the door; they're terrible reasons for someone to sign a contract.

Buyer Proposition #3: "My Service Is "Free" Because the Seller Pays For It

This is one of the most subtle, yet destructive concepts which plagues our entire industry and is something that has led to serious legal disputes surrounding how agents are paid. To tell a prospective buyer not to worry about the cost of your commission is to subliminally suggest that you are nothing more than a parasite looking to latch onto a deal that could have happened without you. You're basically saying that just because your name is the "buyer's agent" line of a contract, that you're entitled to a certain amount of money. Just think about how ironic it is to justify your value as an ethical professional by stating that you have a massive financial conflict of interest at the very beginning of your relationship with the client.

It's kind of like walking into a Dr.'s office for open-heart surgery and them telling you not to worry about their qualifications because the insurance company will pay for it regardless of how well it goes.

This one is a *terrible* look for the industry, and we've got to stop using it.

Become Obsessed with Value

Value has been defined as *"the measure of benefit provided by a good or service."* Your job, in the modern Real Estate reality, is to truly consider and understand the word "benefit" from that definition.

You must be obsessed with the value—or benefit—you provide to the clients who work with you.

It's no longer valuable to simply say you "have access to the MLS" or "Your Mom was my client so you should be too." The internet, and the myriad discount brokerages out there, are providing *transactional* value at prices you'll never be able to compete with. If all you're offering is a popped key box or printed papers, then the iBots have you beat, bud.

In today's world, you must move away from *transactional* value and move toward *emotional* value.

You must appeal to the part of people that the internet doesn't touch. You must connect with their definitions of value in ways that only another *person* can. You must perceive what the other person needs on an emotional level, even when they don't know what it is themselves. What this requires from you is deliberate psychological consideration of the lens through which your customers view the problems *they* face and the solutions *you* offer.

To do this, two things are required. As the agent, you must:
1. Internally understand your own value
2. Externally consider how clients perceive their value

Let's dive into each of these.

Internal: How I Understand My Value

Opposed to the hollow justifications that most agents use when drumming up business, *you* must internally define and understand the substantive value you bring to any transaction.

If you don't understand your value, you can never reasonably expect your client to, either.

Internal understanding of what you bring to the table is the very literal source of the professional confidence you'll need to endure the inevitable rejection we all face.

When prospecting, the average success rate fluctuates somewhere between 1 and 5%, depending on skill and method. This means that—*at best*—95% of the people you talk to when trying to find business are going to reject you with some form of justification for that rejection.

Like a montage from an old "Wile E. Coyote and the Road Runner" cartoon, you will keep getting smashed, kicked, blown up, ran over, incinerated, buried, soaked, and all-out flattened repeatedly. That's just the nature of the job. Now, if after being rejected over and over again, you have no pre-existing foundation of confidence, how long do you think you'll hold up against the Road Runners blows? The simple answer is not long. The statistics give most new agents less than a year.

To resist the blows which will come, you must take the time to really establish internal value—the kind of value so true and real to you that no amount of pain or rejection can take it away.

In like manner, the thing about internal value is that no one can give it to you.

Sure, I could sit here and rattle off a list of 100 things *I* think agents bring to the table. But nearly all of those value items would be situation and person dependent. And, even if I was lucky enough to guess a few correctly, which lined up with your personal situation, they wouldn't last long in your psyche next time you take a few cracks to the chin in the prospecting ring.

Frankly speaking, *you've* got to personally define what you bring to the table, and that process of internal value defining takes *deliberate* time and practice.

The best place to start is by sitting down with a pen and paper and playing a healthy game of devil's advocate with yourself. If you've spent so much as fifteen minutes prospecting, then odds are you've already got a good list of objections to work with.

Write out any reasons for rejection you can think of, and then honestly consider if you could offer value to a person who said one of those things to you.

However, be careful to realize that you can't be all things to all people. Ninety percent of the rejections out there are, to a certain degree, totally valid, and there's not a lot you could do to provide value to that particular person, at that particular time—*and that's ok!*

What we're *not* trying to do here is solve every problem. All you're trying to discover is what your unique value proposition is. If there are 95 problems you can't solve, so be it: that's life.

But what are the 5 problems you're an absolute master at solving?

What are the situations where you excel? When do you shine? When, after you've cashed a commission check, do you look back and say, "Damn, I really earned that money, and my client couldn't be happier."

That's the sweet spot we're trying to find. That's the sweet spot *you're* going to remember.

More than identifying where you struggle, we're trying to highlight the strengths. Then, once you've identified your real, true, enduring internal value proposition, you'll know exactly what types of problems to prospect for, knowing full well that you're completely equipped to serve *that* customer with world-class, value-based, "economic benefit."

External: How Clients Perceive Value

Clients perceive value in 2 distinct ways: **Objectively** and **Subjectively**. Let's look at each one.

Objective Value

Objective: not influenced by personal feelings or opinions in considering and representing facts.

Objective value is the value that translates to most customers in most markets because it doesn't respect any specific person's needs.

It's broad, general, and is more industry-specific than it is seller or customer-specific.

It's less a matter of opinion, and more a matter of fact.

Objective value items are the types of things you would see in those product comparison charts on Amazon. This item has this feature, while "this" comparable item has "this" feature, etc. These absolute value characteristics are directly comparable to other similar products or services.

Speaking in terms of cars (because we're all constantly inundated with their familiar forms of marketing), the classic example of an objective value item would be engine size, towing capacity, the number of cupholders, or the "blah, blah, blah award by J.D. Power and Associates." These items are quantifiable and measurable, with their methods of measurement usually standardized across an industry.

Other examples of objective value would include cellphone storage capacity, bed sheet thread count, TV resolution, appliance energy efficiency ratings, or the mileage warranty that comes with a new set of tires. These things may not mean much to some people, but they're something you can print on a brochure and point at during a sales pitch.

In Real Estate, Objective Value *used* to be the major reason people used an agent to buy or sell a home.

In the early days especially, the primary objective value proposition was the simple fact that you *couldn't* buy or sell a home *without* an agent, so using one—anyone—was a necessary first step.

By simple virtue of the fact there weren't really any other options, the objective value of an agent was that they existed and were readily willing to perform the service for you. Agents, in those days, in a very real sense, were a "ticket-to-ride" the Real Estate train; without an agent, you didn't ride.

Can't get much more objectively valuable than that.

But there were—and still are—other, more granular types of objective value in the Real Estate market.

While the value of these types of sales pitches in the eyes of most clients has been diminished in recent years with the advent of new internet options, they still play a role in the psyches of potential clients when considering hiring an agent.

These objective value propositions include commission rates (particularly for listings), the *ability* to list/access a home on the MLS, yard signs, key box access, average time to sell, average cost of homes sold, average days on market, number of homes sold, the number of years that agent has been in business, or the classically shitty "because you don't have a license and I do" pitch.

These items were once the bread and butter of most listing/sales presentations. Agents would wow customers by pulling their "average days on market" rabbit out of a hat or woo buyer clients with their mystical forbidden key box access. But, these days, in an ever more complex market full of modern value propositions, clients aren't easily persuaded by the old parlor tricks of passed exams or white signs in the sand.

Nope—these days you've got to do a whole helluva lot more than those sorry excuses for a value proposition.

These days you've got to get personal.

These days, you've got to get subjective.

Subjective Value

Subjective: influenced by or based on personal beliefs or feelings, rather than based on facts

Subjective value is the kind of value that's made to order, tailored to fit, and cooked to taste.

In markets dominated by digital leverage and economies of scale, subjective sales is based on shaping your service around the customer, rather than the other way around.

When developing a subjective service, you *listen and learn* based on what you're told, rather than what you think. Subjective value items don't apply to everyone across the board because everyone sees them differently. Less measured than it is perceived, subjective value appeals to the unique characteristics of someone's personality, and the needs and wants that personality dictates.

Subjective value is all about ego; but it's not yours that's most important.

Continuing our car marketing example, why do you think it is that Subaru repeatedly uses dogs and their associated antics in its marketing?

Hint: It's not because they're trying to prove the urinary resistance of the canvas used to make the seats.

What they're doing is appealing to the perceived personality of their target audience.

Subaru people are dog people. Dog people are Subaru people. Doesn't matter that no one really knows what a "dog person" or a "Subaru person" is, all that matters is that *emotionally*, they're the *same* person. Same thing goes for trucks that are "Build Ford Tough," or the Audis that "Drive Perfection."

Rather than being measurable or quantifiable tick marks on a spreadsheet, these are *ideas* being sold as brands; and people are willing to pay lots of money for those branded ideas because they associate them with their own personality—with their own egos.

Starting to sound like a bunch of Freudian mumbo jumbo?

Let's look at it another way:

People are only willing to spend money on things they think they <u>need</u> or <u>want</u>.

With subjective value, we're talking specifically about the *want* part of that sentence—and more specifically—the *why* behind the *want*. People need cars. People don't need Subarus; they want Subarus, at least certain people do. People need trucks, but they don't necessarily *need* a Ford truck, they *want* a Ford truck.

Why do they *want* a Ford instead of a Chevy if they both technically *do* the same thing?

That's a great question. Keep asking it to yourself, because its answer is the reason someone will do business with you instead of some internet broker somewhere.

Like Subarus being sold to "dog people," or Fords being sold to "tough guys," you must market yourself as an agent for _____ clients.

Now, before you start knocking doors with a Labrador in confusion of the example above, allow me to redirect your enthusiasm. What if, instead of seeing your clients as "dog people" or "tough truck guys," you saw them as people who are afraid, overwhelmed, or impractical?

And, going further, what if you created ideas—a personal brand identity—around those people, and the characteristics they may, or may not, know they have?

If you, as a professional, objectively considering the customer you intend to serve, created a brand-persona specially tailored to each example below, what would it look like?

Here's an idea:

Client Type	Your Subjective Branding
Afraid	Confident professional who keeps you safe
Inexperienced	Reassuring guide who has done this before
Excited	Enthusiastic friend who makes sure you don't miss anything
Vain	Executive advisor with a feel for style, trend, and the finer things in life.
Legally Exposed	Experienced escort who knows contracts
Financially Unaware	Help you get qualified so you know how much you can afford
Market Ignorant	Local expert who knows the good deals from the bad ones
Overwhelmed	Reliable butler who's here to make life easier at each step
Overconfident	Humble pragmatist who sees the pitfalls you're unaware of
Stressed	Calming influence that reminds why what we're doing matters
Traditional	Dependable professional who meets expectations with exactness
Modern	Woke professional who understands and communicates real value
Impractical	Relaxed and optimistic voice of reason who relays reality
Uninformed	Educated in the things that will help you get what you want

More than just lip-service, however, you really must embody the brand you're trying to communicate, for true value to be perceived on the client's end.

Rather than just saying you're a confident professional, you must *become* a confident professional. Instead of just stating you're a local expert, you must *develop* your knowledge to where it's obviously authentic. If you sit down in a first meeting with a prospect who's been screwed by a "turn-and-burn" agent in the past you will need to do a lot more than just saying "you can trust me," to convince them.

First, be real. After that, be subjective.

The closer you can get those two things together when considering your client's needs, the sooner you'll set yourself apart as someone who can do the job and be worth every penny in the process.

chapter three

SYMBOLS OF HUMANITY

"When people laugh at Mickey Mouse, it's because he's so human; and that is the secret of his popularity."
- Walt Disney

Internet Real Estate technology is a reality that's here to stay.

Companies like Uber, Google, Amazon, and Netflix have shown how new and innovative technological platforms can disrupt a pre-existing marketplace. Taxis are few and far between, no one uses paper maps anymore, and the concept of renting physical videos has become a nostalgic joke because of how absurd it seems when compared against online streaming.

Innovation and its inevitable advancements are an ever-present part of any marketplace where real money is being made. If money is changing hands, whether it be for products or services, there will always be a young company out there looking to make a name for themselves. Technology creating disruption in a market is as natural and expected as the changing of the seasons. It has always happened, it's happening now, and it will keep happening in the future. It's part of the natural economic cycle.

So, can we please stop pretending like it isn't happening in Real Estate?

Let's admit the obvious:

Companies like Purplebricks, Redfin, Door, Homie, and Zillow have sent shockwaves through our industry in recent years. As I'm sure you're aware, essentially what these companies bring to the marketplace is the option for buyers and sellers to cut an agent out of the equation by buying and selling for dramatically lower costs. They will write contracts, list property, take photos, show homes, and even originate loans for a fraction of the cost of typical agents and lenders. They market themselves as the "smart" alternative, and pose questions such as, "Why would you ever pay an agent $15,000 when we'll do it for $1,500?"

As we've seen these companies sprout in recent years, I've also noticed a peculiar tendency among agents all over the country, regardless which market they belong to:

Like little wizards and witches from the world of Harry Potter, agents treat these industry internet innovators like the Real Estate version of "he who shall not be named." Similar to small children who are terrified of the monsters in their closet, they barricade the door and pull the blanket over their head, pretending that if they don't talk about him (them), then they'll go away. As if Purplebricks or Zillow were some kind of modern-day Voldemort, agents, brokers, and lenders steer clear of ever mentioning them, for fear that admitting their existence somehow makes the "monsters" stronger.

In reality, all these fear-induced heads in the sand do is make our industry seem obviously out of touch—and incredibly insecure.

—and it's that very perception of insecurity these tech companies then use to drive their message home with even greater marketing force. Like a shark smelling blood in the water, they only further highlight their case by pointing out—with ample amounts of witty sarcasm—that all those "greedy agents" are "scared" of missing out on their "fat commission" checks. Then, to make this image of "agents kicking against the pricks" even worse, when potential clients confront agents about these lower-cost alternatives, most Realtors snap back with cheap insults and ignorant jabs which only gives the impression of a scared puppy pretending to be tough after being backed into a corner.

This whole self-imposed technological inferiority complex is just a really bad look for the industry—plain and simple.

My advice to you is to follow a quote which seems to have no clear origin, but offers a philosophy which has transformed the lives of countless entrepreneurs before you:

"Observe the Masses, Then Do the Opposite."

While everyone else is rebelling in paranoid hysteria, I want you to *embrace the very force that scares you.* As if you were the atypical version of a sacred 4-year old version of yourself, walk over to the metaphorical closet, pull down the pile of pillows, and face the thing that scares you most. As many parents, teachers, and philosophers have taught for centuries, once you embrace the fear, it will all at once, lose most of the power it once held over your psyche.

What does this fear facing process look like from a business sense?

It means focusing more on yourself—and your client—than you do on the "monster in the marketplace." It means realizing there's enough fish in the sea to feed everyone...who's willing to work hard and tirelessly focus on meeting the needs and solving the problems—*of the customer*.

Take a lesson from our new techno-compadres and find a pain point in your client's quest for a new home—and solve it. Rather than focusing on your own financial fears or personal pain points, choose instead to obsess yourself with those of your prospects, and there will always be more than enough business to go around.

Now, there are countless different pain points that exist in the lives of our clients. These frustrations, and their associated opportunities for service, are as unique and varied as the people we talk to each day. So, while I will not give you a list of a million-and-one ideas for differentiating yourself, I do want to talk about a single, more generalized concept which is *only going to become more important as technology disrupts our marketplace.*

Walt Disney's White Gloves

Back in 1928, when Walt Disney first conceived and put to screen his genre-defining character Mickey Mouse, he ran into a problem.

In the early days of animation and motion pictures in general, films were restricted to only black and white images. When Walt first released his initial Mickey Mouse film, "Steamboat Willie," he realized that, because Willie's (Micky's) body was black, it was difficult to discern his paws as they motioned and gestured along with the character. The problem was that when the black paws passed in front of the rest of the black body, everything blended together, and viewers couldn't distinguish what the mouse was doing on screen.

The remedy to the problem came roughly one year later with the release of a cartoon entitled "The Opry House." It's in this cartoon that Mickey Mouse is first seen sporting his now iconic wardrobe characteristic: crisp, clean, white gloves.

Now, when Mickey waved, ran, and gestured with his hands, viewers were able to distinguish his hands from the rest of his body. As the years went on, and as characters such as Goofy, Minnie Mouse, and Donald Duck were added to the fold, they also got the now classically Disney white-glove treatment.

Later on, when asked about the reasons for the gloves, Walt revealed an *additional*—subtlety genius—reason he gave Mickey and the other characters gloves:

> *"We didn't want Mickey Mouse to have 'mouse hands,' as he was supposed to be like a human. So, we gave him gloves."*

Robots Don't Wear White Gloves

Consider for a moment the power in Walt's wisdom: "He was supposed to be like a human. So, we gave him gloves."

Unlike the millions of cartoon characters before and after him, Micky Mouse appealed to his audiences because, to them, he was "like a human." Micky was just a simple drawing on a price of paper. But it was the subconscious symbols of his hands that have led audiences to connect with him for generations.

As silly as it may sound, it's those little white *symbols of humanity* that hold the key to differentiating yourself in a Real Estate market increasingly dominated by the forces of technology.

In a world where technology has come up with a thousand ways to make our lives easier, the one thing tech *hasn't* done is connect us to our humanity.

Somewhere, back in the annals of history, genuine human service—performed by actual humans—was a staple in nearly every industry. Real people, serving other real people, did things like pump your gas, cook your meal from scratch, and tailor your clothes to the precise dimensions of your body. Doormen opened doors, milkmen delivered milk, and lunch ladies actually *made* lunch. Before our current age, where technology cuts them out in the name of efficiency, people were once interwoven within the fabric of our economy.

Fast forward to today.

It's a totally different story.

We no longer shop for groceries because they're delivered to our door. When we dine out, whether it's fast food or five stars, most of our meals are pre-packaged or pre-assembled. Clothes come in pre-defined sizes, and heaven help you if you fall somewhere between. Hell, even college educations, for which we pay tens of thousands of dollars, have been watered down to "online" classrooms where instead of lectures presented by a professor, students are treated to virtual chat rooms and "essay upload boxes." These days, it seems like even the most human-centric products and services are becoming more and more automated in the name of minimizing the costs of individual contact.

—and people are subconsciously starving for humanity as a result.

Remember: Observe the masses, then do the opposite.

In an industry becoming obsessed with cutting costs and creating greater efficiency, set yourself apart by giving people the one thing they don't even know they're looking for: *genuine, first-class, white-glove service.* It will have been so long since they've experienced service that you'll probably shock them with what it feels like to actually have another person take the time to consider their needs on an individualized basis.

The interesting thing about the concept of White Glove service is that it shares the same goal of hyper-efficient techno service, in that the primary aim is to make the customer's life easier. *The key difference, however, is how you, as a professional make their life easier.*

Instead of cutting corners, minimizing cost, and removing every barrier to the lowest possible financial cost, focus instead on increasing comfort and *creating an exceptional experience.*

Don't you think it's interesting that the more money people make, the more they spend on things where experience is worth more than just the product or service itself?

Take the airline industry as a perfect example of this phenomenon.

That Boeing 787 airplane is just a tube with wings traveling from point A to point B and has charged several hundred customers a fare for the simple service of being transported. But, not all of those 335 passengers paid the same amount to take what is literally—the same ride.

Everyone takes off at the same time, flies at the same speed, and lands at the same destination. Why then does a coach ticket cost $200 while first class sets you back $2000? Service, baby.

Ironically, in an industry where technological innovation seems to have hit is transportive limits (all airplanes do the same basic thing), the one thing they're forced to differentiate themselves on is the level of service—the experience—you have while on that flight. They don't sell tickets that will get you there faster, but they will sell you a ticket that includes a private room, a hot meal, and even a shower while in flight.

Once sheer tech is no longer a distinguishing factor, simple service is the thing people pay for— and they do so happily.

So, in a Real Estate industry where Purplebricks and Redfin are more than eager to supply the market with cheap-ass coach seats with no legroom, why not accept that, but then position yourself as "the space behind the curtain at the front of the plane?"

Why not offer the Real Estate equivalents of extra-long loungers, complimentary beverages, and any creature comfort your client could ask for? Why not, when the next prospect you talk to brings up the low-cost service of an internet broker, politely and intelligently educate them on the reasons why the costs are so low, and then take the opportunity to explain exactly what you do so differently as a full-service professional?

The simple fact is that in today's market, Realtors are now luxury items.

If a client wants economy service for bottom dollar, they're just not going to call you—and that's OK. But take a lesson from a first-class stewardess, the renowned chef, a custom tailor, the last butler you saw on TV, or Mickey Mouse himself: Serve them.

It's hard to put a price on the cost of our constantly discounted humanity, but if you're willing to pay a little more for it, it can make all the difference in business, and life in general

chapter four

BEING A SALESPERSON

"To be trusted is a greater compliment than being loved."
- George MacDonald

Being a salesperson is a difficult psychological experience—especially for someone who isn't used to it.

I will go full disclosure with you and reveal one aspect of Real Estate I struggled with most, especially at the beginning of my career. Aside from just me, however, it affects every agent, in every market, at every stage in their, career whether or not they know it.

Most agents out there don't even know they're dealing with it. They know they're struggling, but never take the time to put their finger on the source of the friction they're experiencing.

The problem is an instinctual lack of trust.

In 2019, Forbes released its annual list of America's Least Trusted Professions. Real Estate agents remained in their usual spot at the bottom of the list, with only lawyers, used car salesmen, and members of Congress ranking lower. When it comes to the public perceptions of honesty, we're in bad company.

You know you have a problem when bankers rank higher than you do on the ethics scale.

It's very difficult to go to work knowing that most people you'll talk to that day don't trust you. This is particularly true for prospecting, though it can also be true with your established clients. The nature of the business, and of sales in general, is that people don't trust you; more specifically, they don't trust your motives. It's important to note this isn't an indictment on your character, but rather an instinctual, cautionary reflex that nearly all customers have in the modern world.

For decades (and perhaps centuries), customers have been conditioned to question the motives of salespeople.

Since the days of snake oils, people are wary of anything anyone says, so long as there's a financial motive behind it.

When someone knocks on your door, calls you on the phone, or approaches you within 5 seconds of pulling up to the car dealership, your BS meter usually flashes because you know the primary reason that person is engaging with you is because they see you as a potential sale.

Have you ever walked through the mall and seen those kiosks set up in the middle of the main walkways? (Of course, you have! They're everywhere!) Do you ever feel awkward, or even a little anxious, when you see the guy/girl standing there with perfume, or lotion, or a curling iron in their hand watching as you approach so they can attempt to stop you with a question like, "Hey miss, do you want a free facial?" Or "Hello, sir, can I ask you about your exfoliation routine?"

Ninety percent of us never stop to talk to them, and those that do, usually aren't interested in the product but are more afraid as seeming rude if they kept walking. At best, we see these mall bound solicitors as quirky, aggressive retailers; at worst, they're repulsive and intimidating, causing us to make wide circles around their booth while we shield our children.

We don't like them, because we don't trust them. We don't trust them, because we know the only reason they're talking to us is to persuade us to buy their product. And, especially in the modern internet world, we feel that, if their product was really that good, or interesting, or valuable, they wouldn't need to hawk it with such aggression in the middle of the mall. "If I really wanted that," we think, "then I could find it on Amazon, probably with Prime shipping."

It all boils down to trust.

Do I trust you?

Do I trust your product?

Do I trust your price?

Do I trust your service?

Do I trust your motives?

Do I trust giving you my money, believing you will provide me with value in greater, or at least equal, measure?

Those are the questions that underpin all potential customer relationships.

And, the sooner we call out the "Trust Elephant" in the middle of the room, the sooner we'll all be on our way to delivering the goods and services our customers truly need, want, and value.

But, stepping aside from the feelings of the customer for a moment, I want to talk about you, and the effect this innate, automatic lack of trust has on you, as a salesperson.

Being the social creatures we are, we all want to be liked. We all want to be loved. We despise rejection. We (most of us) run from friction, avoid confrontation, and would generally prefer more (rather than less) friends around us. We're genetically programmed to build relationships. We instinctively search out meaningful human connection. When we walk into a room, we all want to be warmly received. We want to be smiled at. We want to be accepted.

But, despite all those warm and fuzzy feelings, we became a salesperson. We got our Real Estate license.

And holy shit, what a wakeup call!

The day before I got my license, I was on the outside of the "Sales Circle" looking in; the day after I got my license, I suddenly saw the world from a different perspective.

Instead of feeling a lack of trust *towards* those used car sales guys, or overly-foundationed make-up mall girls, I had *become* one of them.

It didn't take many outbound phone calls before I realized that the hunted had now become the hunter. The roles had been reversed. Like a cheesy dream sequence from a 1990's Disney channel movie, I saw my head superimposed on the body of a dude wearing skintight pants, trying to sell lotion to mall goers as they walked by.

It was horrifying.

I didn't want to be yelled at. I didn't want to be distrusted.

I just wanted to sell houses and make money.

More than anything, I hated the feeling of people thinking I was trying to deceive them. I hated being hung up on because people thought I was trying to screw them. I hated getting doors slammed in my face because people thought I was trying to run away with their money.

I hated feeling distrusted.

Hard Knocks

I remember one afternoon in particular that drove this home for me.

I was out prospecting by knocking on doors in a quiet neighborhood. I'd chosen the neighborhood because it was slightly older, but was well maintained, and had a reputation for being populated by older residents who may be in the stage of life when they might be thinking about downsizing and simplifying their life.

I was new to the business, probably less than a month in, and was still nervous about knocking doors in "lower-income" areas.

(Ok fine...I was afraid of getting shot, so I decided to knock on old people's doors with pretty lawns).

As I knocked on the door of a classic, red brick rambler with a bird fountain in the front yard and doilies in the windows, a smiling elderly man answered the door. He was probably in his early 80's. His pants were done up around his naval, and he legit smelled of prunes, but he was kind and welcoming. It was almost as if the fact that he was born in an earlier era made him more welcoming to a stranger at his door.

I introduced myself as a local Realtor and asked him how long he'd lived in his home. He responded that he'd lived there 40 years. I smiled with raised eyebrows and told him how rare that is. "You must have a lot of memories in this place," I said. He, in like manner, raised his eyebrows and said, "Oh, yes, lots and lots of those! It's been a wonderful home for us."

He was just starting to share another tidbit about his home when we were both startled by a loud and aggressive "Hey!" shouted from one of the windows upstairs. I nervously looked up and saw the silhouette of another man behind the screen of an open window. He had apparently been listening to our conversation.

"Get the hell out of here you damn parasite!" he screamed.

Before I could even respond, I heard infuriated footsteps pounding down the stairs towards the front porch where the older man and I stood. Expecting a drunk degenerate man who maybe lived in his parent's spare bedroom, I was surprised to see him emerge in a button-down shirt and khakis, with a pair of glasses that made him look like an accountant.

"Who is this guy, Dad, and why are you talking to him!?" he barked.

As his father attempted to speak, the angry accountant stepped in front of him and pulled the screen door shut to protect his father from my presence.

"Let me guess!" he said, in a tone that completely betrayed his otherwise moderate appearance. "You're out here knocking on doors of old folks so you can convince them to sell their house so you can pocket a bunch of cash?"

Trying to calm him down, I confirmed that I was a Real Estate agent, but he interrupted again, "Get the hell off this porch before I call the police! If I wanted to talk to you, I would call you. Get your ass out of here!"

Before I could say anything further (as if I wanted to), he pulled his father back and slammed the interior door.

Through the still open window upstairs, I then heard him very tenderly tell his father, "Dad, you can't just open your door to people like that. They're just trying to take your money. Just don't answer the door if you don't know them, ok?"

I stood there in shock for a few seconds, trying to take in what had just happened. Part of me felt the urge to run as if I had unknowingly just done something terrible and the police were coming for me. It took a few seconds for my brain to reboot enough to replay what had happened, and for me to realize why I had just been chewed out.

That elderly man's son, upon identifying me as a salesperson, immediately reacted as if I was trying to swindle his father out of his home of 40 years. He thought I was dishonest, disingenuous, and deceitful. He saw me as a predator and reacted by protecting his father.

I had chosen that neighborhood that day because I was trying to avoid a bullet to the head.

I took one anyway, at least in a psychological sense.

What stung the most from that experience was that I genuinely had no intention of harming, or deceiving, or taking advantage of that older man in any way. Even the thought of it appalled me. But, for the first time in my life, I had been viewed as and treated like someone who couldn't be trusted. Never before had I been so quickly perceived as someone out to undercut someone else for my own gain, and *I hated the feeling.*

I spent the next several hours driving around trying to reconcile the ambitions of my new career with the sharp and sobering experience I just had on that man's porch.

"Is this how I'm going to be treated for the rest of my career?" I wondered,

"I don't know if I can do this every day."

Frankly, it took a while before I was able to truly understand what happened that day and come to terms with it. Eventually, the lesson I learned, and want to share with you here is this:

In this business, trust is never simply given.

It must be earned. And sometimes, winning that trust can take a very long time.

But the amazing thing is, when people do come to *really* trust you, they reward you with the opposite of the response I got on that doorstep that day.

When people trust you—really, genuinely trust you—they'll defend you, connect you, protect you, incorporate you, remember you, and refer you to everyone they know. And once you develop a network of trusted clients, you'll have more business than you know what to do with.

One of the great ironies in the Real Estate industry is that, while Real Estate agents are a dime a dozen in the eyes of the general public, honest, hardworking, trustworthy agents are incredibly rare and are worth every penny once they're found. They're often treated like family. Once trust is established, instead of doors being slammed in your face, you'll find them being opened as you're invited to family birthday parties and backyard barbecues. You'll get wedding invitations in June and Christmas cards in December.

Hell, I've even seen dogs that initially wanted to take my head off, eventually warm-up and bring me their little dog toys so I could toss them across the backyard.

Trust is a two-sided coin. On one side—without it—you'll get nowhere in the Real Estate business. On the other side, the sincere relationships you build can in many ways be more rewarding than the commission checks themselves.

Stepping into the world of sales can be a surprising experience, especially if you're not used to it's innate social dynamics. Some personality types seem to allow the rain of rejection to roll off their backs a little easier than others. Others seem to feel physical pain with each and every "no."

Anyone can—and does—succeed in Real Estate as soon as they understand the concept and internalize the value of enduring, trust-based, agent-client relationships.

Be genuine in every approach and trustworthy in every deal.

Do that consistently and you'll collect friendships—in addition to your commission checks.

Remember: put people first, paychecks second, and the former will always take care of the latter.

chapter five

THE LAW OF OPPORTUNITY

"Go and look at a stonecutter hammering away at his rock a hundred times without as much as a crack showing. Yet at the hundred and first blow it will split in two, and know it was not that blow that did it, but all that had gone before."
- Jacob Riis

When I was in the middle of Real Estate school, I distinctly remember wondering when we would start talking about how to find clients.

I knew everything there was to know about zoning restrictions, easement laws, and the forms of property ownership, but when the class ended, I found my prospecting knowledge to be profoundly lacking—in the sense it was non-existent.

When I got to the brokerage on my first day, I found myself in a training room with a handful of other new agents who had also just passed their tests. Like a bunch of atheists at a funeral—all dressed up with nowhere to go—we just sat there for an hour wondering what to do next. After the small talk had ended, this little group of clueless newbies shuffled out of the room, one by one, and aimlessly walked out the front lobby doors. Some said they were going to lunch, another said they "had an appointment," and some, I'm not quite sure where they went, because I never saw them again after that morning.

As my first weeks and months went on, I soon learned this "wandering" habit was quite common among all agents in the brokerage, new and experienced alike. I felt like a kid who'd just shown up for the first day of school and realized there were no teachers, so no one actually went to class. A far cry from the bustling and energetic environment I was expecting, I wondered where the hell everyone was, and what—exactly—they did all day.

After a while, I started to put the pieces together.

Essentially, there were 4 categories which every single agent in that brokerage fell into:

1. Directionless New Agents
2. Investors
3. Teams
4. Lone Wolfs

Directionless New Agents: This category is self-explanatory and represented 25% of the brokerage at any given time. It included all the newly licensed Realtors who showed up to the office every morning and had no clear direction on where to go or what to do. During my first 6 weeks, I was firmly a member of this camp. We didn't have desks, or phones, or literally anything other than "new agent" training materials to guide us. As I mentioned, most of these agents drifted away, went on never-ending lunch breaks, and eventually disappeared like the ghosts of forgotten ancestors.

Investors: This group probably represented 15% of the brokerage. These guys were more interested in buying rental property and flipping homes than anything else. Most had been in the business for a while and had long since left the "grunt work" of traditional residential representation behind. These investors were more like construction team managers than they were agents. They usually just sat in their office and counted their money once their property portfolios became large enough.

Teams: Teams, and their associated owners, represented about 50% overall. Their concept, as we'll dissect in more detail later, was a fairly simple pyramid scheme. The team owner would purchase internet leads from Google, distribute them to the "team members" who would call them, generate clientele, and eventually close a small number of deals—a closure rate of roughly 1%. On the few deals which did close, the team owner took an automatic 50% of the commission. The typical agent on these types of teams showed up to the office around 10, called the same batch of 20 leads every morning, went to lunch at 12 pm, and then home for the day by 1. Most never lasted longer than a year.

Lone Wolfs: These folks were the coal mining colonels I talked about earlier. They worked their asses off according to a very specific set of rules, according to a very specific game plan. *They only represented 10% of the brokerage by headcount, but 70% in terms of gross commissions earned.* These men and women were your traditional listing and buying agents who didn't fall for the games and gimmicks of the industry. When they were in the office, there was no bullshit to be had. They locked their doors and worked with a laser focus. When it was time for lunch, they either ate in their office or went with their assistant; they all had assistants. You didn't see them much because they were always in their office or with clients. The one time you would see them was during the quarterly earnings banquet, where they would accept awards for having earned over $250,000 in commissions—*per quarter.*

The Lone Alpha Wolf

David is one of those Lone Wolfs and is someone I admire to this day.

Frankly, I credit him with saving my Real Estate career.

As I mentioned before, after being a new agent in the office for about 12 weeks, I found myself adrift and aimless in a sea of empty beige cubicles. If it wasn't for some sneaky, borderline stalker-ish behavior on my part, I doubt I would have ever met David in person.

After weeks of showing up to the office and re-reading the new agent training materials, I eventually decided to explore the brokerage building one afternoon. Knowing that our brokerage did a lot of business, I knew there must be more work going on beneath the surface.

I walked around various hallways trying to act like I belonged somewhere and that I wasn't merely snooping around like some kind of creeper. Most offices were dark and silent, but at the end of a particular hall, I noticed the light on through the small crack in the doorframe.

It was about 1 pm and the voice behind the door stood out from the silence of the lunch-vacated offices around it. Desperately trying not to get caught, but incredibly interested by the singular sign of Real Estate life behind that door, I walked up and listened through the door frame, praying it wouldn't open.

Ten seconds later, with my ear an inch away from the handle, that damn door opened.

Like the adult version of a 6-year-old stalker who'd just been caught red-handed peeking at the Christmas presents, I jumped up and rapidly tried to think of a valid reason for my existence at that particular place in time. But I drew a blank and just sort of creepily smiled as I quickly stood upright.

The woman who had opened the door was Leslie, David's assistant, and she had a look on her face that said she was about to mace my face and call the cops. I quickly apologized and explained why I was so sheepishly creeping.

Her mouth drew a reserved smile, and she introduced me to David, who, at that point, was thoroughly wondering what the hell was going on. I explained to him that I was a new agent and was just trying to familiarize myself with the brokerage. While I could tell he was busy, and that my intrusion wasn't exactly welcome, his demeanor did soften a little when I told him about my aimless wandering as a newbie.

"I get it; the training here is shit," he said,

"I don't know how these brokers expect anyone to learn anything after they get their license. You haven't had one of those team assholes try to recruit you yet, right?"

Confused at what exactly the question meant, I answered: "No, I don't think so."

"Good," he said, "close the door and sit down."

As I sat, he told me that, while he didn't have time for teaching, he'd be willing to let me watch him prospect—an offer I quickly accepted.

I literally spent the next 3 hours watching the man make phone calls—and I loved every minute of it.

It was like you'd taken a dorky, freshman high school quarterback and gave him a private lesson with Tom Brady in the New England Patriots' practice facility.

I didn't take notes or ask questions. I just watched and tried to absorb what I was seeing. I had literally never witnessed anyone work with such focus in my entire life; I'd certainly never seen it in the corporate world.

He had a standing desk in the corner of the room with a dual-screen computer setup on top. On one screen, he had his CRM (Customer Relationship Management) software; on the other, he had a notepad program with notes about each person he was calling.

For a brief 30 seconds before each call, he would research and refresh himself on the person he was about to dial. When they answered, his masterful conversation skills went to work.

He was direct without being pushy, friendly without being fake, and intelligent without sounding arrogant. He had a specific purpose for each call, which was outlined in each of the notes.

He *never* called with the often used, lame-ass reason of "just calling to check in."

He always had a real purpose for calling.

Some people he called were existing clients, and he provided a courtesy update on the status of their contract. Others were prospects he may have met only once—or even never—and was trying to get to know them in some way. Regardless of who it was on the other end of the call, David was polite and to the point, verbally respecting the other person's time; and then it was on to the next phone call.

For *every single minute* of those entire 3 hours, David meticulously dialed and spoke to person after person, client after client, prospect after prospect. The only pauses occurring were the seconds used to type notes after each call.

Call, note, read, repeat—over, and over, and over, and over, and over again.

It wasn't until later in my career, when I sat down for my own calling sessions, that I appreciated the consistency and focus of what David did.

I don't know if you've ever consistently prospected for 2, 3, or even 4 hours at a time, but it's one thing to talk about it; it's an entirely different thing to do it, and do it well—no interruptions, no distractions, and no excuses. It's a marathon in every sense of the word. There are legitimate reasons most agents don't have the willpower to do it.

After the session, which didn't occur until the digital clock in the room literally displayed "4:00 pm," David turned for the first time since I'd sat down and asked me what I thought. I responded that I thought it was amazing, but that I was tired just watching him.

"How often do you do this?" I asked

"Every day," he replied with a firm smile,

"I do deals because I talk to people, and people only want to talk if you have something other than a sales pitch to talk about. So, I take notes on everyone I meet, every day of the week. Then, I just call them, plant the seed that I'm there to help, and I let the Law of Opportunity do the rest."

"The Law of Opportunity? What's that?" I asked.

He answered,

"The most important thing you never learned in Real Estate school, or that lame-ass new agent guide the brokers gave you:"

"Give Yourself 1,000 Legitimate Opportunities for Success, And Success Will Always Come."

It's important to note that the Law of Opportunity isn't a mathematical or financial law, as much as it is a psychological one.

Contrary to popular belief, it doesn't mean you just throw a bunch of dog shit at the wall to see what sticks.

It's not about ignorantly dropping 1,000 dimes in a slot machine in search of the jackpot.

Most of all, it doesn't mean that thinking 1,000 happy thoughts somehow entitles you to karmic success by means of a "benevolent ethereal universe."

No, what it actually means is:

There is enough inherent opportunity in our naturally abundant economic world for the intelligent entrepreneur to reap in proportion to what they sow.

In other terms: if you consistently work your ass off—according to correct principals—you will succeed—so long as you give yourself enough opportunities to do so.

Creating Opportunity: Your "Modus Operandi"

Your working habits should be centered on the goal of creating as many legitimate opportunities for yourself as possible.

No resistance to any goal can ever hold up to the continued force of 1,000 legitimate opportunities.

Whatever brick wall pops up in your way—and there are a million kinds—it will crumble before your feet if you have the patience and perseverance to attack it with 1,000 true strikes of your opportunity sledgehammer.

The key to the law—and I can't stress this enough—is really being willing to continue striking your brick wall over and over again. Hit, after hit, after hit.

The problem for most people is they all give up after only 5, 10, or maybe 25 swings. Humans—especially humans engaged in Real Estate—are terribly impatient and have the patience of a mouse when success demands the perspective of a giraffe.

If in the heat of your extremity, you believe that the wall will never fall, then common sense says the sooner you stop swinging the better off you'll be, right? I mean, isn't that where the expression "beating your head against the wall" comes from? We fear looking like idiots—to ourselves and others—if we were to continue to expend time, effort, and energy on trying to break down a wall that, in our minds, is destined to stay.

You must create your own chances. And in Real Estate, those chances—those opportunities—are quantified as the number of people you speak to each day.

Nothing happens in Real Estate until you find someone to help.

Houses are not sold in a vacuum. They're not transacted on the stock market. They're attached to people. And your job is to routinely, consistently, tenaciously, legitimately interact with as many of them as you can. From your Uber driver to the checkout person at Chick-Fil-A, to your former classmates, to the policeman who just gave you a ticket (true story!), make sure you're always creating opportunities for yourself by looking to see if you're able to help someone else.

The key to your opportunity creation, of course, if you're like most agents, is focused, <u>intelligent</u> prospecting time.

Now, there's no doubt you're already aware that you need to prospect, so I won't lecture you. There are a thousand others out there who are willing to do that.

However, the one question I want to pose and ask you to consider, is this:

What is it about prospecting that stops you from doing it on a consistent basis?

You know yourself best. You understand your personal pain points better than I do. So, ask yourself, what is it, after a meager 30 minutes of dialing, that causes you to quit? Is it the pain of rejection? Is it the fear of not having all the answers? Is it the monotony of doing the same thing over and over again? Is it feeling like it's not doing any good, so you doubt its effectiveness?

What is it?

Whatever it is for you, I want you to write it down. Define it. Get it out in the open. I want you to turn your internal reservations into external food for thought. Get them out of your brain and into the open where you can dissect them. You'd be amazed how, much of the time, we're not even consciously aware of why we stop doing the things we know we should—especially prospecting.

The most important reason to write down the internal resistances you feel when prospecting is to make you aware that *you are, in fact, feeling that resistance.*

Once you come to grips with those pains and excuses, then you can break them down by developing countermeasures for overcoming them. At the very least, the next time you sit down to prospect for 2, 3, or 4 hours, you'll know the temptations when you see them, *which is the first step in overcoming them.*

It's in these moments of wall destruction doubt that I've noticed a key difference between winners and losers in general. It's something I call *Hope Resiliency*.

Hope Resilience

Hope resiliency is the enduring quality in our character, which tells us to continue with the same zeal and courage, regardless of whether we're on swing #1 or #879.

Instead of feeling fear that the wall will never fall, we instead rely on the inner psychological confidence that comes from *trusting* that 1,000 legitimate strikes of human willpower can topple any wall in our way.

It's not a matter of looking stupid; it's simply a matter of time—and effort.

Further, it's knowing that the goal of wall demolition has very little to do with the nature of the wall, and much more to do with the quality of our strikes—the *legitimate opportunities* we give ourselves. Those with enduring hope resilience focus their efforts on improving each successive swing of opportunity, much more than they do wondering about the integrity of the wall.

Be more concerned with the quality opportunities you create for yourself than you are with the quality of the wall.

One of the hardest things to do when you're tired, or beat down, or discouraged is to be consistent.

Whether it's going to the gym, eating healthy food, studying, knocking on doors, or making phone calls, it seems antithetical to human nature to willingly keep exposing ourselves to the pain of doing things we don't like, or that are uncomfortable for us.

"Swinging sledgehammers" might sound cool at first, but I can tell you from personal experience, swing 99 sucks a whole lot more than swings 1 through 5. Fatigue, boredom, discouragement, and doubt all have a persistent nature about them that seem to constantly eat away at our resolve and determination if we allow them to. No one, regardless of how good or strong they are, feels equally powerful at what they're doing as time wears on, and resources wane. The 4th quarter is always more difficult than the 1st.

Even David, who had developed the habit and skillset of prospecting like no one else I've ever seen, confided that making phone calls for 4 hours each day just plain sucks sometimes.

"I may be good at it, but that doesn't mean I like it," he said.

David, like the rest of us, after having made 127 calls that day, would much rather take a break, crack a Coke, and scroll through Facebook for 15 minutes.

But he doesn't because he understands even the smallest of compromises in his resolve will lead to diminished results over the long term. And the thing that David understands more than most people is that what happens in the long term is vastly more valuable and enjoyable than any momentary gratification that the short term might offer. It's that vision of where he'll be in 6 months that drives him to endure the pain of his current reality.

Long-term gratification is worth infinitely more than short-term gratification.

So, my ask of you is this:

The next time you hear someone talking about the importance of prospecting in a strong Real Estate business, I want you to take a second and reframe that entire idea in your mind.

Instead of seeing prospecting as long, difficult, and rejection dense work that must be done because someone else said it was a good idea, I want you to see it as the very lifeblood of your business.

Rather than counting phone calls, or doors, or emails, or texts, or whatever form of prospecting you use, see these as little, successive moments of opportunity. Instead of memorizing a script or attempting to manipulate a conversation to get an appointment, seek to listen and learn to each person you speak to.

Write down a note. Give a little value. Offer a little kindness. Listen for an *opportunity to help,* and then move on to the next call.

Think of it like you're slowly and deliberately farming the growth of a thousand seeds rather than violently trying to uproot a carrot that isn't ready to be harvested.

Nourish enough opportunities over an adequate amount of time through thorough and persistent work, and you'll see the fruits of the Law of Opportunity unfold in very real and rewarding ways

chapter six

Screw the Guru

"Sometimes the easiest sell in the room is to the salesmen himself."
-Unknown

I'm not sure if you've noticed, but there's an awful lot of people out there who are very interested in telling you how to run your Real Estate business.

There's an entire sub-industry within the greater Real Estate industry whose sole professional purpose is coming up with things to sell to all the agents trying to sell houses.

I call this secondary market the "Guru Market."

The Guru Market is massive and some of its key players may surprise you.

Essentially, the Guru Market comprises any person or company who cares more about selling you something—or profiting off the commissions you make—than they do about any other kind of customer.

The key identifier of a Real Estate Guru, by my definition, is *someone who sees you—the agent—as their primary customer and, as such, their principal source of revenue.*

Now, pointing out the elephant in the room right away, I realize that, by my own definition, you may accuse me of being one of these said Gurus, by the simple virtue of the fact that you paid a few bucks when you bought this book. Let me address this briefly, and then further explain why this chapter is not the literary equivalent of the pot calling the kettle black.

First, to assume that your purchase of this book constitutes a "primary" source of income for me, though a nice thought, is sadly laughable.

I'm not sure how much you know about the book business, but after printing, shipping, and publishing costs, your net contribution to my bank account is around $2.50, a far cry from the hundreds and thousands we'll discuss below.

As a full disclosure, if you couldn't already tell, this book wasn't written to make me a millionaire. It's more like a "cup of coffee for your time," kind of thing.

More to the point, as I mentioned at the beginning, this book was written intending to be more of a collection of thoughts, and an organization of personal experience, than it was something I would tour around the country trying to promote. As I promised, there will be no hook found hidden within these pages persuading you to go to a website, subscribe to a channel, or follow me on social media. <u>My relationship to you as the author of this book, as sad as it may sound, ends with the final page</u>. And while that may seem cold or stupid to some marketing types out there, it's done with a specific purpose. I want you to trust the ideas, and the experiences that surround them, more than you trust me, as some kind of Guru.

Now, with that out of the way, let's talk about the types of Gurus you've doubtless already encountered.

Internal Gurus

Brokers

Let's start with one of the sneakiest Gurus of the entire bunch.

Brokerages, and the Brokers that own them, have a tremendous conflict of interest in the business you do. They have a *major financial* conflict of interest in the commission checks you bring through the door because, in a very literal sense, it's your commission checks that feed their paychecks. In a topsy-turvy way—which I don't think many new agents fully internalize—the agent "tail" very much wags the "brokerage" dog.

I often find it somewhat cute when talking to new agents fresh out of Real Estate school who are innocently preoccupied with finding a brokerage that will "hire" them. Particularly those agents coming from the corporate world, they assume that getting work with a brokerage is like trying to hire on to a Wall Street bank. I've even heard of some agents going so far as to prepare resumes and offer references when seeking to hang their license with a certain brokerage. What they fail to realize is that they, as the agent, should be much more choosey about the merits of the Brokerage, than the Brokerage will be about the qualifications on their resume.

Sometimes, as sad as it may sound, Brokerages are out to find any licensee with a pulse to add to their agent infantry. And, while we may argue the business merits of such a strategy, the point that brokerages are just about as choosy as the Army, should be well taken. If you're a warm body, and willing to sign a contract, odds are, nearly all brokerages out there will welcome you in with open arms.

Because Brokers pay their mortgages with percentages they scrape off the top of your commission checks, you should be very aware of the motives and rhetoric that surround their interactions with you.

Far from the altruistic repositories of wisdom they claim to be, they're often much more interested in quantity, rather than quality, when it comes to the systems they establish to assist you in your deal doing. When sitting in trainings, taking coaching advice, or planning the details of your business, it's best to always carry with you a healthy dose of skepticism which allows you to discern their best interest from your best interest.

Always remember that Brokers aren't bosses. They work for you, not the other way around.

Team Owners

The "Real Estate team" business model is both relatively new and increasingly widespread. It's a concept dreamed up by agents who don't want to open up their own brokerage, but who still feel the itch to scale their income by leveraging the commissions of someone else. The basic idea is this:

An agent within the brokerage creates a "team," or sub-group of agents within the same brokerage, and by so doing, establishes themselves as a "Team Leader" or "Team Owner." These self-declared "leaders" then recruit other agents within the brokerage—typically new agents—with the pitch that they should join their team for more one-on-one training and attention.

Sometimes these team owners may also supply leads (typically buyer leads) to members of their team, who are then expected to work those leads as primary agents. If and when those lead generated deals close, the owner of the team takes a cut of the commission, which is usually somewhere around 50%.

In the mind of the team leader, the ideal model takes shape when 10 to 20 agents work beneath him, working leads he buys off the internet, and he collects 50% of the 20 to 30 commissions which close each month while he sits behind a desk recruiting more new agents.

It should be noted, most of the time, team owners never actually do any deals themselves.

More elaborate versions of this model exist when a team owner solicits the cooperation of other ancillary Real Estate professionals, including lenders, title officers, and home inspectors, who subsidize the cost of the leads, in exchange for a built-in referral pipeline to their businesses. Under this scenario, a complicated web of conflicting financial interests and secretive business dealings develops. Not far from an outright pyramid scheme with brokers at the top, team owners in the middle, and agent-worker-ants at the bottom, this structure usually just funnels money from the peons at the bottom to the masterminds at the top.

This is to say nothing of the fact that it's incredibly disingenuous to the clients generated by the leads who are unknowingly funding a referral machine, which they don't even know exists.

If you're wondering how trust is built, that ain't it.

Trainers, Admins, and Recruiters

This group could be summed up as all of the other folks in a brokerage who are paid salaries and bonuses based on sales or recruiting performance.

Whether it's a trainer standing at the front of a conference room offering "tips" on prospecting, or a recruiter showing up to your Real Estate school graduation looking to sign you onto their roster, their motives are often impure. While I can't speak for every person in every brokerage, let me simply offer the advice, based on personal experience, that many of these brokerage "administrators" haven't seen the front lines of a Real Estate deal in decades, and any advice they may be trying to offer you is ill-informed at best, and downright deceptive at worst.

The question I always like to ask these folks is,

"If you're so good at Real Estate, why did you quit to become a trainer?"

They never respond without stuttering.

External Gurus

Social Media Gurus

The internet has given a stage to anyone who wants it. The only barrier to entry in today's social media world is the 15 minutes it takes to create a YouTube channel. After that, it's as simple as smashing the "upload" button, and anyone can beam their opinions through the ethereal cyberspace, where they conspicuously land on the "recommended videos" feed of YouTube during your morning mid-shit phone scrolling.

You didn't ask for it and you didn't look for it, but there it is, a video promising "10 bulletproof scripts for converting FSBOs" or "How I Went From Being Broke to Owning a Lambo in 90 Days in Real Estate." I'm sure you're familiar with the thumbnails on such videos, which usually include a 20-something looking agent in a fancy suit with their arms raised towards the sky, with a photoshopped cutout of a brightly colored sports car parked in the driveway of a Miami beach house.

And it's not just YouTube; these types of content peddlers are digitally ubiquitous as you move from Facebook to Instagram, to Twitter. Everywhere you look, you'll find promises of secret scripts, motivational origin stories, and the supposed recipes for a million secret sauces which all lead to fame, success, and glory in the Real Estate game.

As I hope you've guessed, the reason these social media gurus have taken the time to build a channel and make a video *isn't* to altruistically unlock the secrets of the universe so you, too, may profit from their wisdom.

Nah.

They're doing it to make money.

Ninety-nine times out of a hundred, if you follow their rhetorical trail for over 10 minutes, you'll find a coaching program, book, training seminar, or monthly membership at the end of the video or at the bottom of the webpage. Less agent, and more marketer, these folks are just out to turn eyeballs into subscriptions and curiosity into coaching programs. They hook you with what seems like bite-sized videos of educational substance, but in reality, are hollow promises constructed with house-of-cards content.

If someone wants to teach you something, that's one thing. But the second that "teacher" starts asking you to do something that involves pulling out your credit card—or clicking a subscribe button—it's time to tune out and get back to working on your business instead of contributing to theirs.

Seminars, Coaching, and Destination Gurus

Ah, the sacred cows of Real Estate education.

From San Diego seminars, to outings in Orlando, we Realtors love the shit out of going on vacation and calling it a "training"—and these gurus know it.

5-star hotels, designer suits, and punch-you-in-the-face portions of perfume all add up to the most educationally enlightening experience one can think of,

amiright?

Look, I've been there; I get the appeal. We all love hanging out on the beach and going to Disneyworld. But let's start seeing these events for what they really are: excuses to spend money under the guise of professional development. I'm sorry to be the robe at a wet t-shirt contest, but these "trainings," and the gurus who put them on are looking to *entertain* you more than they're trying to *educate* you. And, more sinister than just benign entertainment, these gatherings are *specifically calculated* to indoctrinate their captive audiences to a certain set of ideas.

They're meant to bind you to a brand; more specifically, a coaching brand.

Here's how this works:

A guru who's built a name for themselves as an authority figure in the industry contacts brokerages across the country and develops relationships with each broker by sending them swag and making them feel special. In exchange, the guru is offered a "special in-person appearance" at the next brokerage-wide training. Posters and emails featuring the guru's face are distributed everywhere. Excited by the opportunity for a "free" training with the pseudo-celebrity, agents pile into the brokerage training room with pens and paper at the ready. Upon gracing the group with their presence, the guru offers a few recycled pearls of wisdom for 20 minutes before *unfailingly* proceeding to graciously offer a "gift" of one, randomly selected, "free" registration to their upcoming seminar.

Names and email addresses are voraciously scribbled onto entry forms which are then collected at the front of the room, where a lucky winner is drawn.

Feeling like they just won the lottery, they jump up, freak out, and scream to the front of the room while everyone claps. Then, just before the spectacle is about to conclude, the guru motions for the broker to come to the front of the room for some good, old fashioned ego-stroking. Standing at the front, hand in hand, a photo-op fit for a president is framed as the guru validates the broker in front of all the agents. In return, the broker offers one last sales pitch for the guru's upcoming seminar, stating that, "if you sign up today, you'll get a special discounted brokerage rate," with the promise that, "I'll be there. I hope you will, too!"

Three months later at the seminar, as the fervor and excitement of the event have reached a fever pitch, the guru isn't financially satisfied with the simple contributions of $500 per person for registration. So, they advance the narrative to the next phase of the up-sell: Coaching.

To this captive audience of 1,000 agents from around the country, each feeling like they have a special relationship with the guru because of their broker, the guru supports the need to enroll in monthly, focused "coaching." For the "conference only" price of $799 *per month*, you can receive monthly coaching calls from one of the guru's mini gurus, who will help you make sure you don't prove to be the failure your mother-in-law thinks you are.

Just kidding.

Not really.

Half the attendees, having just spent 3 days listening to success story after success story, eagerly and impulsively sign up for coaching at the cloth-draped tables in the back of the room, while the guru, who hasn't done an actual Real Estate deal in four decades, boards their Lear jet.

Not exactly the epitome of educational benevolence, is it?

Get Educated, Not Played

That you're reading this book right now shows you care about expanding your knowledge and increasing your understanding, and I applaud you for it. Mastering your craft and developing your skills are fundamental to any successful professional, especially in Real Estate.

My caution to you is that you learn to ignore the *vast majority* of the gurus out there who claim to have something to tell you.

Ninety-nine percent of the time, they're simply looking to advance their own agenda and pad their own bank account.

Learning who to learn from is a nuanced skill that takes time and experience to develop but can make all the difference in your growth in becoming the person you actually want to become.

If you're going to give someone the incredibly valuable commodity of your personal attention—much less your money—please take 5 seconds to consider *why* it is you've chosen to listen to them.

Instead of gurus, seek mentors.

Look for people so successful at what they do that they don't need to peddle products and subscriptions to make rent.

Actively seek genuine models of success and approach them with humility and respect.

As a general rule, if you're identifying them as a mentor, rather than them identifying you as a customer, you're on the right track.

Be proactive in your learning rather than simply reactive through content consumption.

Seek quality, and you'll be rewarded with quality.

Good information, like good fruit, only comes from trees that have taken the time, and paid the price, to produce it. Search for the best trees when looking for the information upon which you'll build the foundations of your personal and professional life.

Remember, one of the greatest parts of this industry is the chance it offers each of us to be *independent* business owners. Let's not forget that in the search of cheap ideas or compromised content consumption. Build your business into something you can be proud of.

Think for yourself.

Leverage your talents, don't be leveraged by others.

Put on the blinders that allow you to stop being distracted by the voices all around, *and focus on the one voice in the room that actually matters:*

Your client's.

chapter seven

The Three Why's

"He who has a why to live can bear almost any how."
-Friedrich Nietzsche

I wrote this chapter with new agents in mind, but even the most experienced agents will benefit from this type of reflection.

If you're like most people, there are 3 main reasons you became a Real Estate agent:

1. You want to make a lot of money
2. You want to control your schedule
3. You really enjoy working with people

Let's go over each reason in more detail.

Why #1: You Want to Make A Lot of Money

Good for you. Own that. It's not shameful. It's not greedy. Making money is something we all must do in the modern economic world. And, as perhaps you've heard, there is a lot of money to be made in Real Estate. Houses are expensive things. Real Estate agents, mostly, are paid commissions calculated according to percentages. When you mix the word "percentage" with the word "expensive," large commission checks are the result.

The truth is there are very few, if any, other industries that offer the potential to make as much money, as quickly, as does Real Estate. You may have heard the stories of various people getting into the business as fresh newbies in January and are verifiable millionaires by December. That's not hyperbole. That's true. I've literally seen that happen with my own eyes. It happens in every state, in every market, in every brokerage. So, if the prospect of making a million dollars in a year motivates you, take heart, because it's absolutely possible.

Please know, however, that to do so requires tremendous sacrifice. And when I say sacrifice, I mean work. And when I say work, I mean time. And when I say time, I mean your life.

You get the point.

THE THREE WHY'S

The money is indeed out there to be made. But I would suggest to you that 90% of the new agents out there vastly underestimate exactly how much work, how much time, and how much sacrifice is required to make that money. But the great news is if you really put it in, the results do come.

To illustrate this, let me tell you a true story of an 18-year-old kid I worked with in my brokerage.

We'll call him Mitch.

Before Mitch ever graduated High School, he knew he never wanted to work a "normal" job.

He was a pretty skinny kid. Wiry. Scrappy. Not particularly good at sports, but driven inside. Like Tom Brady or LeBron James without the 6-foot frames or athletic ability.

He was obsessed with success, but only if it was on his terms. He read books incessantly. He developed inspirational video playlists on YouTube and kept them on repeat in his car. As soon as he graduated high school, he never wore jeans, only suits.

He didn't come from money. His family was decidedly average. Not rich, not poor. To this day, I don't know if I could tell you exactly where this drive or motivation came from. It just seemed to be a part of his innate identity.

About 6 months before he graduated high school, Mitch decided he would become a Real Estate agent because of the nearly immediate income potential it offered him. In his mind, while all of his 18-year-old classmates would either be sitting in a college class racking up student loans or off smoking a bong somewhere on a beach, he'd be building wealth.

He would take advantage of every second of his youthful head start and begin as soon as the law would allow him. In our state the youngest possible age someone can get their Real Estate license is 18.

So, 6 months before his 18th birthday, Mitch enrolled in Real Estate school. For 6 months, he studied, memorized, read, and prepared. On the day he turned 18, he took his Real Estate exam—literally the same day. He passed on the first try. He had his license the next day. He was on the phones by noon.

I'm not joking.

Now, when I said Mitch was skinny, I mean he was *skinny*.

He's a tiny dude. Probably about 5' 8" tall and weighs a buck-thirty soaking wet.

What this meant was, while the guy had just turned 18, he looked 16. And, I don't know about you, but I don't think that my first inclination after meeting a kid that looked 16, would be to ask him to sell my house. He was fighting an uphill battle from the start.

To appear older and more professional, he wore a suit every day. He had perfect eyesight but bought a $400 pair of glasses with blank glass frames. Glasses make you look smart, right? He learned to speak slowly, with confidence and deliberateness. He didn't use words such as "Dude," "Like," or "Whatever." His goal was to craft the epitome of professionalism out of the frail 18-year-old frame he'd been dealt.

And, it worked.

Between the suits, glasses, and incessant drive to succeed, Mitch cashed over $900,000 in commission checks in his first year.

Not bad for someone who wasn't old enough to buy a Budweiser.

Why #2: You Want to Control Your Schedule

Nothing in life is more valuable than time. Unfortunately, in the corporate world, employers often take advantage of it as the one resource we'll never get back.

I remember when I got my first salaried corporate job. It paid something like $42,000 per year.

It may not sound like much to you, but to me, it felt like I had really made it. When the corporate recruiter called with the job offer, he explained that the expectation was a 40-hour workweek. I wouldn't punch in or out, my pay would just automatically remain the same with each check, according to my salary schedule. Easy enough right?

It didn't take me long to realize why employers use salaried positions.

When you're salaried, your employer owns you.

Legally speaking, when you aren't paid by the hour, you're paid by the job. The thing about hours is that they're definite. They're limited. There's only a certain number of them in the day. The thing about jobs is they're indefinite. Jobs aren't done when the day runs out, or when the sun goes down. Jobs are done when your manager arbitrarily says they are. Hours are grounded in fact; jobs are defined by opinion.

What this meant for me is that, when the recruiter told me they "expected" 40 hours per week, what he meant was that's the *minimum*—the baseline; the number I wasn't to dip below. What he meant was that I would be working *at least* 40 hours per week. More often than not, it was 45, 50, or even 60 hours per week; depending on the project; again, depending on the manager's random opinion.

I can honestly say that never in my life have I been more miserable or felt more like a caged animal. My schedule, and my existence from day-to-day, were dictated by the whims and opinions of a manager.

But what could I do? They owned me. As a salaried employee, as long as I cashed that check every two weeks, I had to play by their rules—the rules of their game.

Good news for you: those rules don't apply in Real Estate.

When you're working in Real Estate, you have the freedom to come and go as you please.

Want to come in early, get some work done, and be out of the office by noon?

Go for it.

Want to come in late and work through the night while the office is quiet? Knock yourself out. Take a 3-hour lunch?

Sure.

Decide to not show up at all?

Totally your call, man; enjoy the back nine.

The first time I experienced this freedom of schedule, I felt like a prisoner set free—literally.

No one was looking over my shoulder. No one measured the time I took to piss. No guilt-ridden looks from people around me if I left early for a preschool graduation. Micromanaging was a distant memory. It's an amazingly liberating way to work.

It's also dangerous.

Want to know why there's so much time flexibility in the Real Estate game?

Because nobody's actually paying you anything.

Basically, you can do whatever you want with your time for the same reason the homeless guy on the corner does:

Technically, you're both unemployed.

No one can tell you what to do because they're not paying you. You might have a broker or a manager, but they're not writing your checks. In this business, you're not paid by the brokerage, the manager, or the corporation. You, my friend, are what's known as an *independent contractor*. You, sweetheart, are paid by the customer—the client. You don't see a dime until a deal is done. No deals, no dollars.

It's the very definition of a double-edged sword.

You may be thinking to yourself, "Duh, I get it. I don't get paid unless I close deals. Everybody knows that."

And, you'd be right—everybody knows that; at least they think they do.

But here's the thing most new agents don't see coming:

That flexible feeling of free time is incredibly intoxicating.

Much like the 21-year-old who's given newfound access to the bottles behind the bar, it's easy to get drunk on you doing whatever you want, whenever you want.

Sure, you may think that you will put your head down, grind, and work like a mule to make your first million. But, I can't tell you how many well-intentioned agents I've seen who, once they realize they can come and go as they please, waste away the hours, weeks, and months of their early days in the business—then are forced to quit because they're broke.

As someone who's experienced both worlds—the corporate drudgery and the independent freedom—I can assure you that schedule flexibility is better in every way.

But I'll warn you now: be careful with it.

Be disciplined.

Watch yourself. Watch your time. Don't get lazy. Don't get soft. It's all too easy to get distracted for a few months, look up, find yourself with no money, and have to go back to Corporate America because you couldn't handle the responsibility of managing your own time.

Be your own boss. It's way better than the alternative.

Why #3: You Really Enjoy Working with People

This is the best "why" of all.

My lovely wife and I have been married for just over 10 years now. One of the great things about marriage is getting the opportunity to dedicate your life to another person. Over the years, as I've progressively opened my heart to my dear wife, she's grown to understand me as a person, on a deep and emotionally intimate level. In like manner, as our love has grown and our relationship matured, my wife's inner secrets and fiercest loyalties have been unfolded to me. Honestly, I never truly understood the meaning of the word loyalty until the day I saw the blessed soul to whom my sweetheart's eternal faithfulness was sworn:

Her hair lady.

Yup. I'm pretty sure my wife would take a bullet for that bitch, as long as she gets the highlights right.

Seriously though, until I met my wife and saw the relationship she has with the woman who cuts her hair, I had absolutely no idea how LOYAL a customer could be to a business owner.

It's truly amazing to witness.

My wife talks about her hair lady like Donald Trump talks about himself. It's a love affair personified.

We have literally planned family vacations, work events, and *even births* around the calendar of this hair lady.

Whatever it takes to make the appointment work, my wife does it. Whatever needs to be done, whatever the sacrifice. To my wife, there's only one being who walks this planet with fingers holy enough to lay hands on her locks.

With that stylist, heaven and earth be damned if anything gets in my wife's way.

And, while this little hair affair often causes me to roll my eyes in exasperation, I've gotta give it to Julia the stylist. When it comes to the business of understanding the needs and wants of her customer, I can't think of anyone who does it better.

She has taken the time and invested the effort to truly know my wife's likes and dislikes. She understands colors, styles, and the latest trends. She knows my wife's hair type, the direction it grows, and which shampoo dries it out too much. I would bet good money you could put a blindfold on Julia, line 5 women up in front of her, and she could tell you which head of hair belonged to my wife based on touch alone.

For my wife, this stylist-client relationship is way past just business. They have literally "been" with each other for years. When my wife sits down in that chair, she doesn't even need to tell Julia what she wants. It was like Julia just knows by osmosis. I'm sure that if my wife came down with the world's worst case of strep throat, but still needed to have her hair cut, she could walk into the salon and they could communicate with nothing more than a wink and a nod in the mirror and my wife would walk out looking like a million bucks.

They are just absolutely, totally in tune with each other.

You can sum up the nature of their relationship in a single word:

Trust.

And it's that trust that has the power to lift any business—especially your Real Estate business—to incredible heights.

If you weren't aware of this before (you should be), tattoo this phrase on your forehead:

In Real Estate, you're not in the business of houses. You're in the business of people.

If you can't talk to people, work with people, approach people, be nice to people, understand people, listen to people, or just generally feel comfortable around people, then you will make a quick exit from this business. People, and the relationships you form with them, are what put food on your table. It's not the houses. It's not the market. It's not the commissions. It's not the brokerage. Your ultimate professional loyalty comes down to the people whom you call clients.

People talk about "knowing your why." It's become somewhat of a buzz-phrase in the industry. While I've never been a fan of buzzwords or buzz-phrases, there's truth in this idea.

You must understand why you've pursued this type of career, at this time in your life, and most importantly, you need to understand *what* you're trying to achieve.

This business will test you.

It's going to be extremely difficult. I guarantee you that one morning you will wake up, head into the office, and you'll get smashed right in the face with a 2X4, figuratively speaking.

You're going to be dazed. You're going to be tired. You will want to quit. It's at that moment that the only thing that will keep you in the ring, keep you making the calls, knocking the doors, and doing the work, will be the *reason* you're doing it. Your reason—your why—is your fuel. It's your impetus; Your force; Your Energy.

Take some time. Think about it. Write it down. Why are you here? Why are you reading this book? Why did you get your license? Why are you trying something that most people don't? Start understanding that—because no one else can understand it for you.

chapter eight

THE RIGHT BUSINESS FOR ME?

"Everyone is a genius. But if you judge a fish by its ability to climb a tree, it will live its whole life believing that it is stupid."

-Unknown

I told you a story earlier about a young, successful agent in my brokerage named Mitch who is producing large amounts of business in a very short amount of time.

Mitch is the definition of driven—perhaps a little obsessed with success. Every thought he thinks and action he takes, from an outsider's perspective, seems calculated towards the very specific purpose of winning, and winning big.

To many people, Mitch is inspiring. To others, however, he's intimidating.

As I mentioned before, at this point in Mitch's career, he's giving it all he's got. Pedal to the medal. Full speed ahead.

At this time in his life, he has the freedom and flexibility to dedicate countless hours each week to the sole purpose of building his business and succeeding at a high level.

But, as many new agents have asked themselves, what if you don't want to be a "Mitch?" What if you don't want, or have the capacity, to burn the candle at both ends? What if you're not motivated by money, or have visions of taking bubble baths in Benjamins?

If you're concerned this business is only for the super-producers putting in 100 hours per week, let me reassure you.

The beautiful thing about Real Estate is that there's room for almost any kind of person, in any kind of life scenario, with any type of personality. You need not be the "Wolf of Wall Street" to make a living as a Real Estate agent.

It's probably best if you aren't.

If you haven't noticed it already, a recurring theme in this book is and will continue to be, the importance of people and the art of meeting their needs.

The thing about people is, there's a lot of different kinds of them out there.

There is, as they say, plenty of fish in the sea—and they all need houses.

These different fish—these different people—like different things. Some fish live in the city and enjoy the concept of paying a stranger to walk their dog. Other fish prefer to live miles away from anyone else and enjoy the smell of cow shit. Some fish have 5 kids and prioritize Parent-Teacher Associations over walkability scores; others won't even consider a home over 1/2 mile from a coffee shop. Some fish are into heavy metal; some are into harmonicas. Some dress up as wizards and fight each other with plastic swords in the park; others just sent the last kid off to college and are looking for something with fewer stairs so their knees ache less while they walk around the house naked eating Cheerios.

You get the point.

There are lots of people out there, and all of them will respond differently to different people—to different agents.

If you're 18 years old, driven to be the #1 agent in the office, and are willing to sacrifice personal time to fill your bank account, there's a place for you.

If you're 35 and looking for a way to supplement the family income while the kids are in school, there's a place for you.

If you're 75, have long since tired of walking around naked whilst eating Cheerios, and are looking for some cash to take a trip to Europe, there's a place for you.

And, of course, if you're a young father who absolutely can't stand another minute of corporate drudgery, who's looking to change his family's financial future, there's a place for you, too.

I will give you 4 brief examples of very different individuals, each of whom I've worked with, to illustrate the point that anyone can succeed in this business, regardless of who you are or where you come from.

Exhibit A: Jennifer

Jenn is a 45-year-old former emergency room nurse. After giving birth to her 3rd child, however, she decided to stay home as a full-time mom. After her youngest child started 1st grade and was in school all day, the quietness of the house started to drive her crazy. At the recommendation of a friend, Jenn got her Real Estate license, hoping to supplement the family finances a bit. Before entering Real Estate, Jenn knew everything there was to know about cells, medications, and helping people feel better; she knew nothing about numbers, spreadsheets, or business in general. She's now been in the business 4 years and makes roughly $100,000 a year, averaging less than 30 hours per workweek.

Jenn succeeds because, more than business or science, she knows—and loves—people.

Exhibit B: Michael

Michael is 36 years old. Eight years ago, he graduated from college with a bachelor's degree in Recreation Management. If you aren't aware (Michael certainly wasn't), it's almost impossible to find a real job with a degree in Recreation Management. While Michael had no job, what he had was $35,000 in student loan debt.

Not a great combo.

To pay some bills, he moved to Snake River, Idaho and joined a river guide company, where he essentially got paid $15 per hour to point out rocks and animals to tourists on the way down the river. When winter rolled around, the tourists went away, and so did the money. He moved back home and found himself broke so he went to work bussing tables.

At the recommendation of a random customer whose table he was working, Michael enrolled in school and got his license.

Michael made $320,000 last year, his 5th in the business.

Michael succeeds because literally every person he meets feels like he's been their best friend for years.

Exhibit C: Mark

I absolutely love Mark's story.

Mark is 6 foot, 8 inches tall and weighs about 170 pounds.

When he walks around it looks like a giant scarecrow stole the clothes from Hagrid's closet. Fashion is to Mark what oil is to water. They don't mix.

Mark is also incredibly shy. He sits in the back of the room, he's not known for looking people in the eye, and public speaking terrifies him.

Not exactly the poster child for a million-dollar agent.

But you know what Mark has?

An incredibly strategic mind mixed with a heart of gold.

Mark is a thinker.

Always more of a social observer rather than an active participant, Mark always thinks before he acts.

After high school, instead of following everyone else to college, he decided to start his own business cleaning office buildings at night. As luck would have it, one of those office buildings housed a Real Estate brokerage. One night while emptying the trash Mark found one of the investment brokers working late. Striking up a conversation, the broker asked him if he'd be willing to clean some of his properties. One thing led to another, and Mike got his license a few months later.

That was 8 years ago. Today, Mark owns 42 rental units, including several duplexes, apartments, and a trailer park.

If you saw him at the gas station, you might mistake him as an awkward guy who plays videogames all night.

You'd never guess his *monthly* revenue approaches six figures.

Exhibit D: Karl

Let's just say that Karl's age is closer to 70 than it is 60.

He used to work part time for the local gas company. He doesn't have a day of formal education beyond high school.

In his early 50's his wife, a school teacher and the primary breadwinner, was injured in an accident and could no longer work. Out of necessity, and against a growing number of medical bills, he got his license as somewhat of a "last resort."

His early years in the business were tough. Technology, and the speed at which the business moved, seemed as if it would force him out. But absent any other option, and by the grace of some very kind and patient brokerage leaders, Karl built a small clientele.

Over time, that small group of clients grew into a medium-sized little business.

During a fundraising drive, one of his grandsons asked if he wanted to sponsor a banner at the high school football field. he did, and it worked. Then he sponsored the baseball team, the soccer team, and, eventually, his smiling face was plastered on every end zone and back fence in the school district.

Today he employs his own team of assistants and "social media" people to run the technological side of things.

What does he do?

Every Saturday morning, like clockwork, he loads up a few of his grandkids in a little red wagon and, armed with flyers noting the schedules of the local sports teams, he knocks on doors and introduces himself as "your neighborhood realtor" while handing them out.

Karl closed over 100 transactions last year.

Beats the hell out of working for the gas company for the rest of your life, don't you think?

Now, considering these (and countless other) success stories, I want to add a point of caution.

You may be tempted to read about the people above and assume that all you have to do is get your license, join a brokerage, and you'll be making 6 figures in 6 months.

Let me slow that roll.

Not only did that quick cash not happen for any of these people, but odds are it will not happen for you.

My point in sharing these stories with you is to illustrate that nearly ANYONE out there can—and does—succeed in Real Estate. Despite educational backgrounds, personality types, personal situations, age, geographies, or any other perceived weakness, this business is full of characters of every shape, size and color.

If you're afraid you're too old, or too shy, or too dumb, or too (insert your particular fear here), let me stop you.

Allow me to encourage you.

Anyone with the right mindset, work ethic, and genuine concern for other people has the potential to thrive. You need not be Chip Gaines, or Donald Trump, or Warren Buffet, or the Property Brothers, or a young hotshot, or a seasoned veteran. You need not be young, or old, or outgoing, or analytical.

The one thing you need to be is dedicated:

Dedicated to working hard.

Dedicated to sticking with it.

Dedicated to learning new things.

And, dedicated to serving your clients in the most uniquely genuine way that only you can.

Do that, and you'll be amazed with what can happen.

chapter nine

EKG Income

"If you are not willing to risk the unusual, you will have to settle for the ordinary."
- Jim Rohn

Have you heard of an Electrocardiogram before?

Even if you haven't heard that medical term, you're probably familiar with what one is from TV. An Electrocardiogram, or an EKG, is a visual graph that measures and displays the electrical activity associated with a person's heartbeat. These are the machines in those medical shows that make the "beep, beep, beep" sound. If the person's heart rate increases, the frequency of the beeps goes up as well. Then, as most often happens during TV medical dramas, someone eventually dies and the "beep, beep" turns into one long "beeeeeeeeeep," followed by the on-screen Dr. wiping the sweat off his forehead and declaring time of death. Short beeps mean the blood is flowing; One long beep means you're dead.

What the hell does an EKG have to do with Real Estate?

I like to chalk this concept up under the "things new agents think they understand, but really don't," category.

The standard pattern of an EKG serves as a perfect visual representation of the financial and emotional rhythms of the Real Estate business.

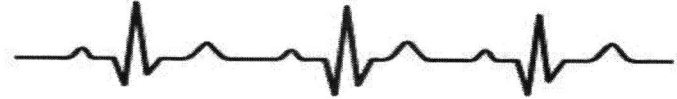

Real Estate income is not "normal" income.

There's nothing scheduled or guaranteed about the money we make. Close five transactions one month, get a spike. Close zero deals next month, but still have to pay your mortgage, get a dip. It seems one of the rules of life that the bills are ever present; unfortunately, in Real Estate, the income is not.

Truth is, you don't understand this concept and the effect it has on you until you experience it first hand, particularly over an extended period.

I thought I grasped what it meant to work all week and not be guaranteed any income at the end. But, let me assure you, at the end of the first month, when I was tired, working late, and showing up bright and early every morning, it really sucked to realize that the nugget dipper at McDonald's made more than me. At least they got paid *something*. I put in 50 hours and all I had to show for it was gas receipts.

We all like to think that our mood, enthusiasm, and resolve will remain constant amid changes and struggles.

But it doesn't.

It's similar to the experience you may have had when you walk up to the treadmill for the first time in 6 months.

You just had an energy drink, your headphones are pumping some sweet jams, and you naively think you will run for 60 minutes straight. It's only after the first 10 minutes, and while you're enduring the sensation of your lungs melting inside you, that you realize you may have bitten off more than you can chew.

Your eyes, as they say, were bigger than your stomach.

Continuing the metaphor, it's usually no big deal to admit defeat, hit the stop button, and sheepishly admit that we weren't prepared for what we said we would do.

In that scenario, the only consequence of our over-eagerness is running to the bathroom to blow chunks before we slunk into the comfy, inclined seat of a recumbent bike.

Yes, hopping off the treadmill after an embarking on an ill-prepared workout is usually pretty forgiving.

The Real Estate journey, however, is a much less forgiving trip once the train has left the station. There's no red financial bailout button for a bad month.

The bills constantly come due; the deals don't always come through.

Be Prepared—Seriously

The skill you must master, and the struggle you must prepare for, is *how you will mentally deal with the financial droughts that will inevitably come.* To do this requires deliberate financial and psychological preparation.

Financial Preparation

You wouldn't start a road trip without a full tank of gas. Don't start your Real Estate career without enough savings to cover at least 6 months' worth of expenses.

I get it, believe me. Changing careers is exciting. Getting your license and building your business is an incredibly fun and hopeful time. You want to jump in with both feet and hit the ground running when you can. And I encourage you to do that, but don't be so enthusiastic and emotional that you quit your job on Friday, start Real Estate on Monday, and have no money in the bank.

Odds are you won't close a deal during your first, second, or even third month. Most new agents forget that even when you find a client, then find a home, then negotiate pricing, and finally get under contract/escrow, it still takes 30-60 days, on average, to close that deal and get paid. So, even if you start day one of your Real Estate career with a piping hot client in hand, you're still at least one month away from any kind of actual payday.

I like to think of the beginning of your Real Estate career like a giant boulder sitting at the top of a snow-covered mountain.

That boulder is huge, heavy, and frozen to the ground. During the first months of your career you have to start digging around the base of it, brush the snow off, leverage all your bodyweight, and exert every ounce of force you have just to get it to roll an inch. After all of your work, sweat, and energy spent to get the boulder to move that first inch, the *last* thing you want to happen is for your financial resources to run out and you have to stop pushing, just as the damned rock is starting to move!

But this happens all the time!

I've seen it over and over again.

Well-intentioned agents start, financially unprepared though they may be, and think they'll just work "extra" hard to close their first few deals "real quick" and they'll have enough to pay the bills in a few weeks.

It just doesn't work that way.

Real Estate deals take time. New Real Estate careers, in particular, are like a pump that needs to be primed.

This ain't a microwave kinda deal, sweet cheeks!

Just like waiting for an egg to mature before it can hatch, your prospecting, clients, and their eventual deals can't be rushed to fit the frantic timeframe of your constantly diminishing bank account.

Trust me on this one. Put some money away, reduce your monthly expenses, give yourself a buffer—THEN start pushing.

Now, when that boulder rolls, you won't have to worry about stopping. You can dig your heals even deeper into the dirt, push harder, build that momentum, and get that big, stubborn, gravity-laden rock moving down the hill with an ever-increasing amount of speed.

Wise is the agent who begins their career from a position of power, rather than one of weakness.

Psychological Preparation

Every day you wake up in the business of Real Estate, you're unemployed, remember?

That might sound scary or anxiety inducing, but it's a philosophy I encourage you to adopt early in your own business. Nothing is owed to you in this industry. Every time you close a deal, there's never a promise of the next deal.

There's uncertainty. There's worry. There's Anxiety. It's part of the gig. Riskiness comes with the territory.

Understand that now.

It will help you succeed later.

As you embark along this career path, you must do so with the clear and sobering understanding that every day will be a risk/reward proposition.

You must internalize that *there is a very specific economic reason there's such tremendous income potential* in the business of Real Estate. The potential is great because the risk is great. There's no such thing as a safe, reliable, or predictable harbor in which you can camp out while you consistently cash checks.

Skydiving—the act of jumping out of a plane—is exciting and adrenaline-pumping because there's a risk you could die. The vast majority of the population will never know the view or experience the sensation of free-falling from 20,000 feet because they aren't willing to trade the risk for the experience.

In a very similar sense, the vast majority of laborers out there will never know what it feels like to rope in a deal, negotiate it to perfection, and cash a $20,000 check at the end because the risk of *not* cashing that check is simply too great.

The reason I'm driving this point home so hard is that I've watched too many naive Real Estate "skydivers" jump out of a plane without ever putting on their parachute. Most don't even know they're 20,000 feet above the ground. Then, without taking 5 minutes to consider the reality of their situation, they leap out of the door because someone told them to, and they try and figure it out on the way down.

Frankly, many don't even know they're falling until just before they hit the ground.

Maybe you're only 18 years old and the only real financial obligations you have are your cellphone and Netflix account. If so, jumping into the business with no preparation and falling flat on your financial face may not seem like much of a big deal. You won't freak out if you go through your first 3 months without a deal because, hey, let's be honest, no one's going to starve because of it. So you might be late on your Verizon bill; who cares, right?

I would argue, however, that the vast majority of us out there *do* have significant financial responsibilities, and with those responsibilities, come significant risk. For the rest of us, no deals after 3 months, and a mortgage hanging over our head, will cause us to freak out, lose focus, and bail from the business long before we've given it the time necessary for success.

My advice? Don't let the risks of this business surprise-bite you in the ass 3 months into your career.

Right now, at the very start, come to grips with the uncertainty. Face the precariousness.

Gain full comprehension of what you're about to do, and then, build your business with confidence upon the foundation of full disclosure and defeated ignorance.

Keep your EKG machine beeping. Don't get too excited when the beeps speed up, don't fall into the depths of despair when things slow down.

On the 1st day of the month, you may have 8 deals in escrow, and it looks like a huge month is in store. By the 25th, they could all be dead and there's not a dime to show for it. That's literally happened to me. Things will spike, things will dip, then things will average out.

Don't fear the failure potential; just accept it and keep going. The only time you're truly dead is when you quit. Amid all the uncertainty, one of the beautiful things about this business is that no one, other than yourself, can declare you dead.

Remember: Short beeps mean the blood is flowing; One long beep means you're dead.

Prepare yourself now for the reality of dry deals and high bills. Arrange your brain to deal with the stress so you don't shit a brick when the deal you're counting on for your car payment falls out of escrow. Compose yourself with the expectation that the buyer's financing will fall through and all of the work you put into the deal will feel worthless. Steady your resolve with the knowledge that appraisals will come in low, interest rates rise, and markets cool.

Shit will happen. Shit has always happened. And yes, my friend, shit will continue to happen, even as you aspire to the highest ranks of Real Estate royalty.

There's a line from classic literature which sums this idea up well: *"The arrow seen before cometh less rudely."*

The psychological arrows are going to come. See them coming now, so you can succeed in spite of them.

chapter ten

Assumptions and Expectations

"The customer's perception is your reality."
-Kate Zabriskie

Whether they know it or not, people—clients—have expectations.

Inside each of their psyches rests an assumption that certain things will happen in certain ways.

When they pull up to the drive-through at their local Golden Arches, they expect the double quarter pounder with cheese to taste a certain way. The fries, since they were a young child, have always come with a certain amount of salt, combined with a certain texture on their tongue. The coke is supposed to be cold—always. The bag should have 4-5 napkins, and everything should smell a certain way once unwrapped. They know and expect this because it's happened just this way countless times before.

The expectation is an internal, unconscious forecast of what should be, based on what has been.

In a similar, yet slightly different fashion, once a young bride-to-be finally has a shiny engagement ring on her ring finger, she begins planning the big day she's spent her entire life dreaming about. She's clipped the magazines, read the blogs, and attended countless other weddings as either a flower girl or bridesmaid.

Though she's never actually been the bride herself, years of watching others, and anticipating her own walk down the aisle, have shaped an expectation of how things should be for her once her turn finally comes around.

Both examples are instances of expectations needing to be met to lead to satisfaction. The difference between the two is experience. One example is based on a history of personal experience, while the other is fostered by repeated, 3rd person observations.

Whether it's French fries and Coke's or table settings and flowers, people condition themselves to anticipate things in powerfully emotional ways.

There's something about things happening just the way you expect that brings about a certain feeling of satisfaction.

Say what you want about spontaneity, but human beings love predictability. It makes us feel good. It validates our thoughts, feelings, and impressions. Biting into a Snickers bar and tasting sweet instead of sour is something that no one ever complains about.

Expectations Are Born from Stereotypes

Like them or not, stereotypes are very powerful things.

As humans, our assumptions, based on the archetypes around us, dictate how we interact with people places and things. You've heard of the notion you only ever get one first impression, right? Well, what do you think first impressions are based on? If you think we only judge each other by the nature of our character, I hate to break it to you, but you're wrong.

We judge, we assume, and we *expect* based first on *what we see*. It's what we see, hear, and feel that forms our impression. Then, it's our impression that forms our expectation. Those expectations are then shaped by our past experience.

I see a Lamborghini; I expect it to be fast.

I see a person at Target wearing a red polo and khaki pants; I expect them to know which aisle the lightbulbs are on.

I see a person wearing a large, white coat that extends down to their calves with a stethoscope around their neck; I expect them to be knowledgeable about colds, coughs, and broken bones.

As a Real Estate agent, you *must understand the stereotype you represent to the people you interact with.*

Going further, you must be aware of the expectations they have of you, based on what/who they think you are—*and what they think you want from them.*

When you call someone on the phone and introduce yourself as "Mike from ABC Realty Brokerage," their mind immediately forms a response based on the conversational stimulus you've given them.

ASSUMPTIONS AND EXPECTATIONS

We call this a "knee jerk" reaction.

Their response will be a mixture of three things:

1. Their impression of who they think you are
2. Their assumption of what they think you want from them
3. The context of their current situation, relative to the points above

For example, let's say you're knocking on doors prospecting for new listings. You're a male, wearing khaki pants and a polo shirt, with a shiny name tag pinned over your chest. It's summertime, 90 degrees outside, and you're by yourself. You're also holding a handful of fliers.

You knock on the door. A middle-aged gentleman opens the door. You smile and wave, "Hello, sir!"

You don't know this man's name is Robert. He's 65 years old and recently divorced. He has 4 kids, none of whom live with him anymore, and he works a job he despises as a bookkeeper for a local shipping company.

He's lived in that home for the past 10 years but has been thinking about moving on to something smaller now that it's just him and the kids are gone. A few years back, one of his co-worker's son's became a real estate agent after dropping out of college. He only lasted 3 months in the business before taking up driving Uber to pay rent. With much of his newfound free time, Robert has been watching a lot of HGTV shows where investors buy old homes intending to fix and flip them for large profits. By nature, Robert is grumpy, introverted, and no-nonsense. He was just sitting down to a freshly microwaved hot dog and can of Coke when you knocked on his door.

Based on what you now know about Robert, what do you think he thinks about you, based on his two second first impression?

1. His impression of who he thinks you are:

"This guy must be selling something. People don't knock on doors unless they're selling something. Cookies. Houses. Religion. People at my door are always selling something."

2. His assumption of what he thinks you want from him:

"He's wearing a polo, maybe he wants to cut my grass. No, grass guys don't wear khakis or name tags. This guy looks like he's got some money. He's probably a flipper. He wants my house. He wants to buy my house and flip it. He probably thinks I'm an old sucker who will sell it for cheap.

3. His expectation, based the context of his current situation, formed by what he sees/thinks:

"Investors are Real-it-tors, aren't they? Real Estate agents. I hate Real Estate agents. They're all a bunch of bums looking for a quick buck from honest people. Mike's kid…yeah, like Mike's kid. Deadbeat kid who passes a test and wants 6% of my house. This kid's trying to screw me."

Unfortunately, you haven't even gotten through the screen door yet and Robert thinks he's got you all figured out.

Ironically enough, if you pull away his stereotyped impression of you, Robert could really use your help. He doesn't know it yet, but you could make his life better by getting him into a better home for his situation, and probably even put a decent amount of cash in his pocket.

Your job, more than anything else, is to learn how to cut through Robert's inaccurate first impression and help him see the truth in the service you're offering, and how it can benefit him.

It sounds simple, but it can take years to master.

Not Just for First Impressions

It's easy to understand the importance of assumptions, impressions, and expectations when we're talking about meeting people for the first time.

But, the true power in understanding what drives the notions of our customers becomes more evident during the later stages of a relationship.

Let's assume that you've found a customer who's agreed to work with you. You've shaken hands, smiled, and you've got their list of wants and needs.

Over the past 3 months, you've been out with them nearly every Saturday showing them various homes you've found on the MLS.

For one reason or another, each house just doesn't quite seem to fit what they're looking for. On one, the backyard is too small. On another, the street is too busy. Last week they thought they absolutely loved the one on Pinebrook Dr. until they heard the dogs barking in the next yard over.

You've spent hours each week making appointments and hours each weekend showing the houses. These people are personally responsible for at least 500 miles on your odometer. You're tired, but keep pushing. All you need is one yes and you'll be under contract, you tell yourself.

Finally, at the end of another long Saturday, it happens.

You show them a 3 bed, 2 bath bungalow on a tree-lined street that just became available last night. You're the first buyers in the door, and the seller is motivated. Your buyers love the house! No red flags, the price is right, and they want to make an offer!

"Great!" You say, "I'll head to the office right now and get started on the paperwork."

Not so fast.

"Oh," they respond awkwardly,

"Actually, my mom's friend has a daughter who's an agent. She told us to find the right house then she'd help us with the offer. Thanks so much for all your help, but we're all set!"

You can barely pick your mouth up off the floor before they've hopped into their car and driven away.

There you are, standing under the perfect oak tree, in front of the perfect house, on the perfect street: 3 months, countless hours, 500 miles, and nothing to show for it.

Sorry to say it, but you just got bit in the ass by the false expectation fly.

Damn it. That house even had a tire swing.

Simultaneous Ass-Umptions

Now, before you think I gave you that example as a reason to get an Exclusive Buyer Agency Agreement signed, let me stop you.

(Of course, you should never show any home to any buyer without a written agreement in place first; but that's not the point here.)

The real point is, in the above example, *you* were operating under assumption A, and *your buyers* were operating under assumption B.

Assumption A: These particular prospective home buyers have never spoken to any other agent and are solely committed to working with you because you've met with them several times and have shaken hands.

Assumption B: This really nice Real Estate guy sure has been helpful in helping us open the doors on these houses. We're not really sure why he's there, but he keeps making appointments and he has access to those little key boxes. We've been planning on using my mom's friend as our agent for over a year, but we just assumed this guy worked for the sellers of these houses.

Again, the point here isn't about contracts, handshakes, or other agents. There were 2 assumptions operating at the same time, but neither party was aware that any assumption, *other than their own*, existed.

It's called human nature and we all do it.

Whether it's contracts, prospecting, showings, listings, lender relationships, family deals, phone calls, advertising, taxes, transaction coordinators, licensing, title reps, team members, buyers, sellers, coaches, property managers, or brokers, the lesson is this:

Always be aware of hidden assumptions and their related expectations.

As a rule of thumb, remember:

Without communication, most of the time what you're thinking *isn't* what the other person is thinking.

The longer both of you operate under false assumptions, the more trouble, friction, and pain will result later.

As the agent, you're the leader. It's your job to make yourself aware, as much as possible, of your client's assumptions.

You do this by asking questions. Lots and lots of questions. And then *listening intently to the answers.* If something doesn't quite make sense, ask another follow-up question. Keep going until you understand, as much as you're able, what's going on beneath the surface of that person's mind.

Like anything else in business, the more information you have, especially regarding what your clients are thinking, only strengthens your ability to serve them.

Information is power.

Information on unspoken assumptions is game-changing.

chapter eleven

BEWARE OF MOTIVATION

"Commitment means staying loyal to what you said you were going to do long after the mood you said it in has left you."
- Unknown

I'm telling you right here, right now; master this skill and you'll change your life:

Don't Let Your Mood Control Your Work.

I readily admit that I'm no behavioral psychologist, but I can virtually guarantee you that 90% of the people in your social circle aren't consciously aware of the influence their mood is having on them and the work they do.

The Power of Mood

Much like the weather being universal in its influence across the human family, our moods, and the effect they have on our behavior, fundamentally shape our perception of the world.

Like a bunch of little sailors in tiny boats at sea, we curse the waves while remaining ignorant of the wind. You can't really blame us, though, because becoming aware of the weather—our mood—is more difficult than it seems.

From the moment we wake up, to the moment we fall asleep each night, we're under the influence of how we feel, whether it's good or bad, positive or negative. These feelings—or states of mind—can be physical, mental, spiritual, social, or any combination of a million factors in our environments. Eating gas station sushi before bed, or learning that your home is being foreclosed on, make for equally shitty morning moods, even though one is gastrointestinal and the other is financial.

The fact is there are a million variables coming at us like a 6th-grade snowball fight every single day. These "mood making" experiences come so fast, and so often, that we eventually get used to them and, over time, become unaware of their influence over us.

String enough days, weeks, and months together and the waters of mood, along with our habits that form around them, become truly muddy. Eventually, we fail to distinguish internal mood-makers from external mood-makers and subconsciously throw our hands up in the air, giving in to the idea that we're merely the victim of our circumstances.

It's bullshit, but we believe it, because of the power of repetition.

But the influence of mood goes both ways—negative *and positive*. Ironically, it's the positive mood-makers we seem most unaware of, especially when it comes to how they negatively influence our behavior.

This "positive mood resulting in negative behavior" phenomenon is never more apparent than on New Year's Eve when the world is symbolically (and alcoholically) intoxicated with the visions of grandeur associated with starting a new year.

You know, all the "new year, new me" bullshit that runs through all our cerebrums on January 1st.

We're all going to read 20 books, get new jobs, eat only salads, and get down to 6% body fat. As if, driven by nothing more than the stroke of a clock, our decades-long behavioral patterns will suddenly cease and we will become new, insanely fit creatures driven by discipline instead of indulgence. In those moments, our moods—and ambitions—are artificially inflated to dangerous levels of self-deceit which inevitably set us up for failure—and the self-loathing which follows close behind.

Why is this?

Because the foundations of enduring behavior change can never be built on the Styrofoam bricks of random calendar dates, temporary dopamine spikes, or the visceral images of toned abs seen on midnight infomercials.

Arbitrarily emotional highs are always tempting us to write behavioral checks our willpower accounts have no hope of cashing.

If you've ever been to a Real Estate sales seminar, then I'm sure you're familiar with this experience. I won't name names, but I trust you know the type of event I'm referring to:

5,000 agents dressed to the nines gather in the conference room of a swanky hotel in some tropical location. Loud music thumps, people clap along to the beat, lighting effects dance around the room, and the guru, with their hands in the air, takes the stage. People scream, and whistles of adoration echo against the walls as this minor Real Estate celebrity feigns humble acknowledgment of their affection.

During the next 3 days, the audience is treated to highly energetic injections of motivational mumbo jumbo.

Panels of success symbols are called up on stage to reminisce on the millions they've made. Talk of sports cars, beach homes, and endless deal pipelines are bragged about ad nauseam. People scribble down pages of notes, jump up in the air, and drink themselves into mildly responsible levels of public intoxication.

At the end of the "conference," every soul ~~stumbling~~ floating out of that ballroom room feels like they're on top of the world and are only weeks away from being their brokerage's next top agent. Emotions are running high, bars have run out of booze, and the "motivation" meter is about to explode.

Two weeks later, back in the beige reality of their stand-up cubicle, they're officially feeling the effects of the hangover of half-baked commitment.

Indeed, cheap motivation is the least enduring kind.

But where, then, does lasting motivation come from?

Nowhere.

Because it doesn't exist.

Like Santa Claus himself, the idea that any of us will ride a wave of emotional momentum to the shores of enduring accomplishment might be fun to believe in for a little while, but at some point, we must grow up and realize that nothing comes from nothing and emotional highs don't last forever.

Seminars, infomercials, honeymoons, first dates, new car smells, and the novelty of Taylor Swift's new song eventually fade away, and the emotional spike we once felt—like a sugar rush—comes back to a baseline where the laws of sacrifice, discipline, and insulin still apply.

The nature of mood is that it changes. The trick is not to let your mood—or motivation level—dictate the work you do, or the level of commitment you employ.

You must not allow your headspace to dictate your workplace.

The best way to do this is to set your goals and decide where you want to go when you're as close to emotionally sober as you can possibly be.

No one knows yourself, your situation, your past, your strengths, and your weaknesses better than you. The last thing you want is for you to deceive your own self with delusion and half-assed commitment when you're making personal promises about what you want to achieve in life.

Now, there's something else that's important to point out here:

Just because I'm asking you not to rely on mood, emotions, or motivation when setting goals and doing your work, doesn't mean I'm asking you to abandon hope or put away positive thinking. On the contrary, I'm trying to help you understand the difference between the two—the difference between shallow excitement and enduring vision.

Being able to dream, think, see, and visualize where you want to go, and the rewards that you'll find there, are fundamental to the willpower needed to endure through tough times. Strategic vision, powered by a gritty attitude, combined with the willingness to work your ass off, are exactly the kinds of traits that eat mere "motivation" for lunch.

In a sense, I'm asking you to think more like the cross between a coal miner and a colonel.

I want your hands dirty and calloused from the daily, committed work, and I want your mind sharp and your strategy defined with exactly how to get there. I want you to understand that your path to success will undoubtedly feature brick wall after brick wall and that the Real Estate business is going to continuously crack your jaw with the swing of a metaphorical 2x4.

There will be opposition. There will be emotional low points. It's during these times that your job is to remember your vision and keep "shoveling" that damn coal.

It's the grit you exhibit while in the pit that counts tenfold more than the cheap motivational shit which eventually leads you to quit.

And how can you remember to put away meager motivation in the name of real commitment? It's both and uncomfortable simple:

Once you've set your goals with a clear mind and you're going about the business of your daily work, *start paying attention to how you feel.* Write it down if you have to. The beautiful thing about commitment is that it constantly reminds you how important it is—*every time you don't feel like doing something you know you should do.*

The pain of discipline is the trigger that tells you you're on the right path.

Set a goal to do 30 deals this year?

Great.

You'll be reminded when it matters most next time you feel like skipping out on prospecting after the first 10 rejections.

Knock on 100 doors, 20 open, and 20 people tell you to kick rocks; it's the *pain* of embarking on the *next* 100 doors in 90-degree heat that *reminds* you you're still committed. In those extreme moments, forging discipline and winning willpower is worth much more than any potential prospect behind a door.

It's when you want to do something the least that discipline says you should do it most.

Pushing through pain, breaking down barriers, and enduring through difficulty are the prices to be paid to experience the enduring joys of accomplishment. After you've strung a few successes together, you'll experience the real fun. Like fresh lemonade to an exhausted coal miner's lips, the fruits of committed labor become intoxicating in the soberest sense of the word.

Realizing that your sacrifice has led to success will generate the sensation of traction which inevitably leads to satisfaction. Traction satisfaction will then only reinforce your healthy habits of determination the next time you find yourself in the pit. Work hard and push through barriers enough times, and you'll find yourself in the self-efficacious headspace of a winner who knows exactly how they got there.

That, my friend, is worth infinitely more than any temporary dose of "motivation" could ever offer.

chapter twelve

HOMES ARE EMOTIONAL THINGS

*Human beings are emotional first. You have to find their emotions.
You have to let yourself feel emotion in order to do this work.*
- Joe Rohde

A gents are often tempted to treat homes like any other commodity that's routinely bought and sold.

This, of course, is understandable to a certain extent, because of the volume and frequency with which we engage in Real Estate deals. Do anything day in, day out, especially in a professional sense, and whatever that thing is, it can become routine, sterile, and transactional. This is a well-documented phenomenon with physicians, for example.

But, unlike doctors, your professional success is based solely on the *experience* your client has while working with you.

You must always retain in remembrance the experience your client is having, at each step. And, if you do—if you truly develop the habit of thinking about what your client is thinking—you'll soon find yourself aware of how very differently clients view homes.

You'll find that, to them, homes more closely resemble the family dog than they do a building of wood and nails—at least *in an emotional sense*.

These structures, more than just conglomerations of bricks, sticks, and stones, are both the literal and symbolic centers of human life.

People bring their brand-new babies through those doors, put handprints in fresh cement, and etch their children's height into door frames. They spend weekends painting rooms, planting flowers, and pruning shrubs. They sing in the shower, dance in the living room, and have sex on the kitchen table. They paint Easter eggs, light off fireworks, and open Christmas presents. It's where meals are cooked, fires are lit,

HOMES ARE EMOTIONAL THINGS

and bread is broken. Between barbecues in the back yard and birthday candles being blown out, homes serve as the arenas where the seasons of life are celebrated.

Beyond just acting as the repositories of life experiences, houses are also primary sources of human protection. They keep the rain out and the heat in. Warm in the winter, cool in the summer, and calm when it's windy, homes are literally a refuge from the storm. Locks keep intruders out, fences keep the kids in, and garages keep the cars protected. Homes, and their comforting walls, are the very symbol of safety in a world that routinely makes people afraid.

And it's that fear, along with every other emotion in the book, that you'll find yourself working *with* and *against* as you attempt to navigate these overly emotional creatures we call humans, through buying and selling the very structures which have literally *come to define their lives*

A "What Not to Do" Story

I want to tell you about Amy.

Her name still raises my cortisol levels.

Amy is a young mother of 3 ~~terrifying~~ adorable little girls, all under the age of 10. Having been through some unfortunate relationships in her younger years, she found herself as a single mom, with no fatherly financial support, before she turned 30.

She is an extremely hard worker, having climbed the ranks to become a department manager at Wal-Mart during the day while cleaning offices in the evening when her mom watches the kids. She'd never formally graduated high school and had been dealt some pretty shitty cards by life's dealer, but through the sheer force of tenacity, she had built a comfortable life for her girls.

I had only been in the business a few months when I met Amy. Her landlord had just increased her rent to an insane amount. It was so incredibly high that Amy knew she could purchase a home and still save significant money each month. So, we sat down, and I started my usual process of asking her about how many bedrooms and bathrooms she wanted.

All seemed to go well until the day we started looking at homes.

When we met at the first house, I was surprised when I reached out to shake her hand and she just nodded without unfolding her arms.

"Okay..." I thought, "maybe she's sick."

As we walked into the house, I attempted to very casually explain the layout and give her some of the basic info, including beds, baths, and total square footage.

However, as soon as she entered the house, it was as if I didn't exist.

She completely ignored the fact that I was speaking and took a hard left down the hallway and into the bedrooms. Standing in the kitchen with a newly bruised ego and pissed off disposition, I simply waited for her to complete her silent tour. When she emerged from her self-guided walkabout she simply said,

"This isn't the one."

When I asked her to clarify what she didn't like, she just said, "I don't really know."

"Well, maybe if you'd let me F'ing help you, then you'd know!" I said.

To myself.

In my mind.

Then I thought of my mortgage payment, forced a smile, and said,

"No worries! Let's go see the next one!"

I spent the rest of the morning muttering mixtures of verbal malice as I drove between homes like a disgruntled Homer Simpson turned Realtor.

I'd open a door, and she'd ignore my existence, I'd think about how badly I needed the commission check, wait for her to tell me it wasn't the one, and then drive to the next house on the list. It was literally the most passive-aggressive day of my entire life. And before you point out the idiocy of my situation, let me remind you I had been in the business for less than 90 days. This, by far, was not my finest moment.

I was starving for a deal.

Because of my financial desperation, I was unknowingly guilty of grumbling below deck while Amy drove the proverbial "ship." Desperate and inexperienced, I ~~furiously~~ patiently waited in the crew's quarters, sending up the coordinates to the next island while Amy and her emotionally driven hands were at the wheel.

I thought she was just being a jerk.

In reality, she was petrified.

What I didn't know—because I never *really* asked—was that *Amy was afraid.*

Like most people, when fear floods their brain, the primitive, reptilian brain takes hold of the controls and poor choices are always the result. When this happens, and fear tightens its grip on the mind, reality fades away and the smokescreen of anxiety rises in its place.

Unfortunately for both of us, I was too busy hyperventilating about commissions and printing our MLS sheets to ever take the time to recognize the reasons behind her fear, much less actually do something about it.

It was only after 6 months, countless showings, 500 miles on the odometer, and *5 buyer-canceled contracts* that I finally realized what was happening:

Amy was terrified of buying a "bad" house.

Up to that point in her life, in her mind, Amy had made only bad choices. She'd trusted the wrong people. She'd followed false hopes. She'd been burned, broken, abandoned with 3 little girls, and was paralyzed for deciding where she and her girls would finally put down roots. With a history full of every conceivable form of fear, distrust, and anti-safety, Amy was desperately searching for a refuge from the storms of the past.

What she couldn't see, however, was how her fear was shaping her impression of each and every home she set foot in.

That should have been where I stepped in to help. There I was, right smack-dab in the middle of this swirling storm of emotion, the dumb, desperate agent so focused on closing the deal I couldn't see how to help the client right in front of me. My commission breath was so bad at this point that all of the mouthwash in the world wouldn't have been enough to cleanse my intention and focus my attention.

She didn't trust me; and her cold, arm-folded silent treatments were simply an outward manifestation of an inner panic surrounding the thought of potentially purchasing the "wrong" house. It was a full-blown lizard brain situation, but once you understood where she was coming from, could you really blame her?

This all eventually came to a head after she requested to back out of our 5th formalized contract prior to the expiration of the Due Diligence deadline. At that point I told her I felt it would be best if we went our separate ways and that I could no longer be her agent. She agreed.

After 2 weeks of silence, my phone rang while I was out to lunch with some agents from my office. By then, Amy's name and home buying saga had become quite the comedic tale for my agent colleagues, and they broke into shocked laughter when her name, yet again, popped up on my phone.

Against my better judgment, I answered.

She explained that her mother, who I had met at a few of the showings, called her and pointed out the fear she was experiencing. Her mother, being the one person Amy trusted, calmed the fear just enough for the panic to subdue, and for the lizard-brain to fade away.

For the first time, she apologized and asked if the most recent home was still available. It was. I begged the selling agent to give us another chance, which she surprisingly did, and Amy closed 30 days later.

After the papers were signed, as we stood up from the closing table, she finally extended her hand,

"Thank you," she said with tears in her eyes,

"Honestly, thank you. It's been a really hard year for me, and buying a house was just something I thought I was going to screw up. I was just afraid I'd make a bad choice. Thank you for being patient with me."

While it ended well enough, there was a valuable lesson to be learned:

Amy's deal had closed despite me, rather than because of me.

It wasn't my fault that Amy had fears about buying a house, but it was my fault I didn't take the time to really listen to my client and solve her problems.

At the Mercy of The Illogical

I'm not sure if you've ever found yourself in a situation like Amy's, but if you have, then you were treated to a large and lovely dose of something I like to call "Illogical Frustration."

Essentially what this is, is the exacerbation that comes when trying to help someone accomplish a task, but they are routinely resistant to your help for what seems like entirely illogical reasons.

In Amy's case, I showed her no less than 50 homes over a 6 month period of time. I'm here to tell you that at least 75% of those homes were wonderful, safe, and quality options which would have served her family well. But the problem was that I was assuming Amy saw the world (the houses) the same way I did. I had ignorantly taken my experience and market understanding for granted, and just assumed that she was seeing—and judging—things as I was. And, worse than simply taking my knowledge for granted, I failed to put myself into her headspace, so I could see the homes through Amy's "lenses."

So, metaphorically speaking, let's say there was a pair of "glasses" Amy was wearing, which I was to borrow for a few minutes.

If I took the glasses from her nose and placed them on mine, what would I have seen?

Well, for starters, I *wouldn't* have seen square footage numbers, costs per square foot, or recent comparable sales. No, what those glasses *would* have shown me is the size of the bedrooms and whether or not they were suitable to share between kids. I would have seen the cracks in the foundation, and, not knowing they were just plaster cracks, I would have been afraid the house was about to crumble. I would have seen where the Christmas tree would go, and whether or not there was room for a full dining table in the kitchen, because moms don't like food in the front room. I would have noticed the condition of neighbor's yards and the sound levels at night. I would have been freaked out by an old water heater because I have no idea how to even light one.

Most of all, I would have judged each house by its ability for me, as a single mom, to give my girls a safe place to grow up—a place that would be fondly looked back on for years to come.

Those lenses would have shown me that the home buying process is driven much more by sentimentality than by practicality.

You've gotta understand: houses define people's lives like nothing else.

Their perceptions, hopes, dreams, aspirations, and even financial considerations, aren't always grounded on the firm footings of generally accepted Real Estate reality.

Rather than becoming frustrated with the illogical, take a deep breath, step back for 5 mental seconds, and consider the situation from the alternate, more emotional, viewpoint.

Take the time to understand your client's value system. Whenever they tell you what they want, *always* ask the follow-up question of *why;* and then ask *why* again, again, and again. The thing about emotions, especially the sources and reasons behind them, is that they're never simply surface level.

Human motivations, and their associated sentiments, are rooted in years and years of experience, pain, hope, and other personally historical validations.

Your job, as much as you're able, is to subtly ask, dig, and inquire into the reasons people want what they want, and then do everything in your power to help them find it. And remember, to you, it may not always make much sense. But then again, as crazy as it sounds, *sometimes when things sound weird to you, but light up the face of the client, it's then that you know you're on the right path.*

You've heard the adage that "the customer is always right."

Well, this isn't because they know all the answers.

Frankly, it's actually the opposite that makes that statement true.

With customer service—especially emotional customer service—the "right" answers to the questions aren't in a book or a manual; they're in the brain, the life history, and the psyche of the person asking the question. And, they can only be unlocked by someone—some agent—willing and emotionally intelligent enough to patiently listen to and solve the problems.

One of the worst mistakes you can make is to assume that a house is just a house.

chapter thirteen

The Tobacco Of Time

"Time is the coin of your life. It is the only coin you have, and only you can determine how it's spent. Be careful lest you let other people spend it for you."
-Carl Sandburg

According to recent studies, the average person only lives about 78 years.

Some live longer, but many live less. If we round up to make ourselves feel better, even 80 years doesn't seem like much time. At least not to me, considering how quickly the first 40% of my life has gone.

But, even if we get the entire 80 years, you might be surprised how little of those years are actually spent, you know—living.

Of those assumed 80 years, according to recent studies, the average modern life is spent in these activities:

- 28.3 years sleeping
- 12.2 years at work
- 11 years of "screen time"
- 4.5 years eating
- 3.5 years on education
- 2.5 years on grooming
- 1.4 years exercising
- 1.3 years socializing
- 1.3 years commuting

Add all that up and subtract it from our hopeful balance of 80 years, and it only leaves us with *roughly 9 years of self-directed living.*

It's these precious marginal hours of autonomy that literally come to define our lives.

Now, if you're like me, when you read that list, you compare it against your own life and wonder if you really do spend so much of your life on routine and run-of-the-mill activities.

The sad fact is that we probably do.

We all must sleep, eat, work, and bathe. We get stuck in traffic, take the train, and wait in the security line at the airport. And, last I checked, it was still impossible to gain knowledge by osmosis, so schooling, college, and education in general, will continue to require our attention.

But there is one item on that list—quite high on the list actually—which we do control, and which doesn't seem as necessary:

Screen Time.

More specifically, the internet.

That one there, my friend, that simple, inconspicuous, 3rd little item on the list, will revolutionize your life and your business—if you learn to control it.

The internet is the single, most universally transformative tool that mankind has ever developed. It provides us the ability to store, share, and process limitless amounts of information which, only a short time ago, seemed literally impossible.

But, as the information universe has suddenly been distilled upon our fingertips, it has brought with it a subtle and serious side-effect:

The internet has become history's most efficient thief of the most valuable resource any of us will over possess—our time.

For building your Real Estate business—or doing literally any worthwhile thing in life—*the simplest, yet most effective advice I can give you is to minimize (or preferably eliminate) every minute of unnecessary, time-sucking time spent on your phone, tablet, or web browser.*

The internet can propel you to incredible success and it can mire your days into the total of a wasted life.

Eliminate unnecessary screen time use, and you'll automatically qualify yourself in the top 5% in efficiency and time management.

Everyone wastes time online. If you choose not to, you'll automatically qualify for the exclusive high-producers club, by simple virtue of the fact that you now have more time than anyone else around you—especially your competitors.

Eliminating wasteful screen time is an automatic and instant game-changer.

But it takes discipline. Lots of discipline.

The great paradox of our modern, internet-driven world, is that the web is the most necessary, yet evil, success-determining factor we encounter on a daily, hourly, and minute-by-minute basis.

More subtle than a payday loan shark, the internet doesn't charge interest by percentage. Rather, it slowly drains the lifeblood of our days by soaking up our attention through a steady deduction of seconds and minutes of screen time— time which we never get back.

That's the best way to think about the internet—as a bank.

Like any banker, it's willing to provide you with resources you wouldn't have otherwise, but it does so in exchange for compensation, particularly over time.

The internet will always be willing to provide the transformational resource of information utility but does so in exchange for the increasingly invaluable commodity of your personal attention. *Never underestimate the value of your personal attention.* These days, in a very literal sense, it's worth much more than just cash. Just because a website doesn't require your credit card number to login doesn't mean you aren't paying anything. In the digital ecosystem beaming from behind our screens, your two eyeballs are worth significantly more than the sixteen digits on your credit card.

And that's specifically what the internet machine does — keep your eyeballs on the screen. When we constantly interact with a "machine" that was built to monopolize (and monetize) attention, breaking free from its gravitational pull is easier said than done

—but will change your life.

For winning at business, this idea is so obvious, yet so elusive, all at once. The obviousness, yet ignorance, of wasted screen time reminds me of a photo I once saw hanging on the wall of my Dr's office.

The image, entitled "An Intimate Portrait of The Tour De France," is a black and white image from 1927 showing riders Julien Vervaecke and Maurice Geldhof, smoking cigarettes while competing in the legendary bike race.

THE TOBACCO OF TIME

I'm not sure what those men knew about the dangerous effects of smoking cigarettes. But, even without the advantage of modern medicine, they must have known that smoking while trying to perform at their athletic peak probably wasn't the best idea. There must have been something in the back of their minds that said, "You know, Julien, maybe sucking large amounts of tobacco and tar into your lungs while trying to ride hundreds of miles isn't the best idea."

They must have known that, at the very least, it wasn't helping; At the very worst, it was slowly killing them.

With success in Real Estate or any other business, scrolling through your damn phone looking at memes, or watching YouTube videos, or checking sports scores, or snap chatting your friend's cousin's sister, or even the pseudo-responsible task of news reading—

—is the modern time management equivalent of taking a long, slow drag on a cigarette while trying to win a competitive race.

From a productivity standpoint, it makes absolutely no sense.

But for whatever reason, we do it anyway, every single day.

We know it's probably not the best idea, and we don't feel great when we do it, but everyone around us has their head in their phones too, so it's not that big of a deal, right?

Wrong.

It is a big deal.

It's a massive deal.

It's the most overlooked deal in the whole damn Real Estate game.

It's such a big deal, in fact, that if you stopped stupidly scrolling and absent-mindlessly clicking, you be amazed how many more *actual Real Estate Deals you'd do!*

Look, I'm not trying to yell at you like some parent trying to get their kid to play less Fortnite. I'm not trying to convince you to turn in your iPhone for a flip phone or transition back to CDs or cassette tapes. I fully understand how truly engrained technology—and the internet—has become in the fabric of our lives. But it's that very duality of "good internet" vs. "bad internet" that makes it so easy to transition from one to another without even knowing it.

Think about it, how often have you sat down at your computer to get some work done, maybe even prospect a little, when only 3 minutes into your work you're unknowingly pulled away into wasted time? For me at least, it happens so frequently, and so subconsciously, that at times it feels like I don't even have control over my own "digital willpower."

I know we never admit these kinds of things publicly, but in the honesty of our own minds *we've all* looked up at the clock after screwing around on the internet all morning to find that it's 2 pm and the only actual thing we accomplished thus far was the bowel movement initiated by our morning caffeine.

Now, before you fold your arms and look away, scoffing at how ridiculous that sounds, just stop—because we've all done it, sweetie. Yes, even your shit stinks. And, unless I've missed my guess, your face was probably staring at your phone whilst taking said shit, so my point is only further proven.

Speaking from experience, I remember one day in particular when I suddenly became infuriatingly conscious of all the subliminal digital surfing I was doing.

I had come into the office that day with the clear and distinct "goals" of taking care of administrative work from 8-9 am, resolving lender financing issues from 9-10 am, and prospecting past clients for an upcoming client appreciation event from 10-2 pm. *I had just spent $5,000* to reserve an entire movie theater for the event, and had even shelled out extra to have popcorn and drinks provided. It was the end of the year, and I pulled out all the financial stops to provide something valuable and memorable for my clients.

But then I decided I'd just check the news real quick.

While doing so I came across a story in the sports section updating the new national ranking for our local college football team. As a loyal fan, I inherently clicked.

While reviewing the rankings, I had the thought that "the team's having a really good year, I should go to next Saturday's game." So, I went to the ticketing website. After feeling like the tickets and associated fees there were too pricey, I decided to check the online classifieds for secondhand tickets. As "luck" would have it, there was an ad listed just 12 minutes before, with someone selling a crazy good pair of tickets for an "incredible" price (one of those "my loss, your gain" kind of deals). Realizing my "good timing" in checking the site, I immediately texted the owner of the ad. He responded within 30 seconds saying he already had 5 people offering to buy the tickets, but that none of them were available to meet until "after work."

Smiling a stupidly self-congratulatory smile, I thought to myself, "Sucks for those guys who work 9-5 jobs. I'm an independent agent who don't need no man to tell me what to do," and my egotistical little thumbs pounded out the response, "I can meet you in 10 minutes." The ad poster agreed, and I immediately left for my car.

I got back to the office 60 minutes later with tickets in hand and $120 less in my Venmo account.

Knowing that no "good deal" is actually a good deal until it's gloated about to those around you, I scrambled inside the brokerage, up the stairs, past my office, and into another office of one of the agents who I knew would appreciate the transcendence of my newly acquired tickets. After externally validating how awesome my "deal" was, he offered up the reminder that the game to which I had just bought tickets was a "blackout" game, and I would need to wear black clothing to fit in with the atmosphere in the stadium.

Never one to procrastinate an impulse purchase, I scurried back to the laptop in my office and surfed the web, looking for some sweet black merch with which to adorn my deal-seeking self. And, naturally, knowing that all the best online deals are won using coupon codes, I spent no less than 45 minutes Googling variations of the phrase, "Nike Outlet Coupon Code."

At long last, I found a glorious little code that saved me a grand total of 10%, amounting to a monetary value of less than $10 off. After clicking "buy now," and responsibly waiting 10 minutes for the confirmation email to arrive, I looked up at the clock.

It was 3:35 pm.

I had started reading the news at 7:45 am.

In that moment of internet time-sucking realization, I literally felt sick to my stomach.

Only days before I had shelled out *five thousand dollars* as an investment in my business success in the coming year, but

I had just slipped into an internet black hole searching for deals that "saved" me something like 75 bucks, all things considered.

More than money wasted, it was time wasted. And, more than just time wasted, I reeled in shock with how quickly *and subconsciously* I had allowed myself to mindlessly throw away my day. Hell, when I was gleefully responding that I could "be there in 10 minutes" I was even weirdly proud of my "professional flexibility" that allowed me to do so.

A fool and his time were soon parted.

I went to that football game the following Saturday, and my team won that night. But, sitting there in the stands, wearing my newly purchased black Nike hoodie, I couldn't help my mind from being preoccupied with the lapses in judgment that had led to those tickets.

It was an enduring wake-up call for me.

I don't know what your internet time-sucking stories are, but you do; we all have them.

Big or small, long or short, the web is simply too ubiquitous for anyone to truly remain outside its influence at all times. Whether your personal brand of this "tobacco of time" is Social Media Marlboros, Reading the News Newports, or eCommerce Camels, we've all taken unhealthy, repeated drags on the subconscious cigarettes of Big Internet.

My recommendation for you, as with any smoker, is rather than attempting to quit cold turkey (and do all your work with notepads and calculators), simply start by becoming more aware of what you're *allowing yourself* to pay attention to.

It helps to watch your small habits each day, especially when those habits are spurred by environmental cues. Next time you open your laptop and click on the familiar Chrome or Safari icons, do you find your fingers almost automatically typing in the first 3 letters of the word INStagram or FACebook and waiting for the address bar to auto-populate where you're habitually heading?

When you're in the bathroom stall, try keeping your phone in your pocket. Seriously, we joke about this, but it's as if we've forgotten how to loosen our sphincters without the visual stimulation of an iPhone in our face.

Try thinking, rather than scrolling, next time nature calls.

When you find yourself early to an appointment or waiting for a meeting to begin, why not resist the urge to purge YouTube for cat videos, and, instead, take in 15 minutes of a book—made of paper? Last I checked, Barnes and Noble still hasn't figured out a way to print an ad with the shoes you looked at 6 months ago, in the book you're reading today. Take advantage of that increasingly rare kind of informational sanctuary in a world that seems to want to predict your every digital move.

Most of all, make your working hours as productively sacred as possible.

Use a website blocker if you need to. Set rules for yourself and follow them. There's no need to check social media 12 times before lunch. There is, however, a need to speak to 12 people about your ability to better their life with your services. When it's time to prospect, have a zero-tolerance policy for intrusions and interruptions—especially the self-imposed ones.

When the time comes around to take a break, read the news, or to make that Amazon order, do so consciously and with purpose. It may sound stupid or trivial, but set a timer and put hard limits on the time you spend gazing at pixels. Awareness is always the first step.

In an industry that seems to have more agents clamoring for its financial fruits every year, do yourself a favor and put forth the professional discipline which most of them aren't even aware they're lacking.

Give yourself the advantage of time.

Reclaim the resource of a strictly followed schedule.

Gain the advantage that comes with rooting out the weakness that your competitors don't even know they have.

Time is the only resource any of us really have.

Make the most of it, and you'll be well on your way to making the most of this business.

chapter fourteen

Forget To Be Afraid

"Thinking will not overcome fear, but action will."
-W. Clement Stone

Sometimes people succeed simply because they didn't know they weren't supposed to.

In that sense, ignorance, rather than being bliss, is a blinder that allows you to focus on what really matters.

Let me tell you about Kyrylo.

Kyrylo was born in the Ukraine, formerly of the Soviet Union, in the mid-1980's. Kyrylo's family was beyond poor, and never knew any home larger than a two-bedroom apartment stacked among a thousand others in a giant, concrete apartment building rising into a grey sky. His father worked as a diesel mechanic and barely made enough to buy bread and beans. His mother worked for a screen-printing shop at night, printing graphics on uniforms.

Growing up in the place he did, there was never any sort of economic promise that offered hope for anything more than the type of menial labor his parents performed.

As a child, he never really hoped for any trade or profession in particular. Like his parents, he just wanted to basically survive. In his mind, if you had a warm home, carbohydrates on the table, and the occasional pair of shoes, you were considered in good shape. It was all about the end, rather than the means, that he cared about most. It didn't matter if you were a mechanic, a factory worker, or a farmer; you were just happy to "be" something. As a child dreaming dreams about the future, he didn't have the luxury of being picky.

So, when he moved to the United States at 19, he wasn't expecting much.

About 6 months after arriving in the U.S., Kyrylo waited tables at an upscale hotel downtown. To him, still only recently removed from the dire circumstances of his childhood, this job that allowed him to wear a white shirt and tie, *and* paid him for doing so, seemed like an occupational dream come true. Literally, he told me he planned on bussing those tables for the rest of his life and doing so will a grateful heart.

Then, one day while taking the trash out to a dumpster in the parking lot, he glimpsed the most beautiful thing he'd ever seen:

A 2001 Mercedes Benz S55 AMG.

Two men in business suits had just stepped out of it and were handing keys to the valet.

Like a sheltered 12-year-old boy seeing a woman in a bikini for the first time, Kyrylo just stood there with his garbage bag in one hand and stared.

"It was like I couldn't help myself," he said.

"I had never seen a piece of metal that was so beautiful and elegant before. I was mesmerized."

He was so obviously car horny that the driver of the Benz couldn't help but notice and offered a smile and waved as he walked inside the hotel.

That would have been the end of the story were it not that after dumping the trash, changing his underwear, and coming back inside, Kyrylo found his table assignment to be none other than the one which belonged to the man who drove the Mercedes.

Standing up straight and proudly marching over to the table with a proper waiter's cloth draped over his left arm, he introduced himself with a thick Slavic accent.

During the next 90 minutes, Kyrylo offered the 2 dining men an exceptional, 5-star dinner experience. At the end of the dinner, as Kyrylo was removing the empty plates from the table, one man commented that they couldn't help but notice Kyrylo admiring the car earlier in the evening. Kyrylo somewhat bashfully admitted that it was the first time he'd seen a car like that before. This eventually led to a brief conversation about his recent immigration to the States and acquiring his "dream job" waiting tables.

Kyrylo didn't know it, but his candor and positive attitude had made an impression.

After parting pleasantries were exchanged and the men had left, Kyrylo returned to the table to finish clearing the plates. What he found in the payment envelope, along with a generous tip, was a sturdy business card emblazoned with silver lettering which read "Broker."

Turning the card around, he found a handwritten message on the back:

"Thanks for taking care of us tonight. Give me a call if you want to know how I bought my Benz."

Looking around as if he may have perhaps done something wrong, but also like a kid who'd just found a secret treasure map worth much more than the tip itself, he slipped the card into his pocket and tried to restrain a smile as he went about his work for the rest of the night.

The next day, using the phone in the back of the restaurant's kitchen, Kyrylo called the number on the card. The man answered, thanked Kyrylo again for the great service, and asked him to stop by his office that afternoon. It was pretty far away, but Kyrylo decided he could take the train.

His life would never be the same.

Five years later, he was up on stage in a high-end, tasteful custom suit. He was being recognized at a large brokerage event, accepting an achievement award for outstanding contributions to customer service. He occupied a corner office and drove a very familiar-looking Mercedes Benz. Kyrylo was closing roughly 40 transactions per year and was making more than most surgeons. There, at the front of the room, I watched as the original "Benz driver" put his arm around Kyrylo and, with emotion in his voice, re-told the story about the night he'd received exceptional customer service from a waiter with a Russian accent.

Now, if you think the moral of that story is a rags to riches recounting of a nice kid from the Ukraine, you're wrong.

Because I haven't told you about the most incredible thing about Kyrylo yet.

The amazing thing about Kyrylo is because of the unique circumstances in his background,

He was never aware of the fear most agents are pre-conditioned to feel.

The innocent economic ignorance of his upbringing allowed him to operate without the inhibitions that almost any other new agent has.

In his mind, he'd already won the lottery the day he got that job waiting tables in a white shirt. When the gods of providence *further* gifted him with that business card, in his mind, it was as if he was playing with house money.

He had nothing to lose, everything to gain, and because of that, *absolutely no fear*.

It's amazing what you can do when you're not afraid.

I met Kyrylo for the first time roughly 18 months after he'd taken that train ride to meet the broker. He was doing well in the business but was definitely still new to the game. As I worked among him and the other new-ish agents, it was enlightening to see how he *processed things so differently than the rest of us*.

When the market was up in the spring, he didn't care, because he didn't know it was "up." When things slowed down around Christmas, his level of effort and focus stayed the same, because he didn't know about the idea of a "holiday slowdown." In a broader sense, when people worried about rising prices, falling prices, hot markets, cold markets, or technological competition, he didn't care, because he didn't know enough about those things to fear them.

So, he just kept working.

All he knew—*and trusted*—was that "the man that drove the Benz" told him to talk to people, make his calls, manage his contracts, and deliver the same kind of service to them, that he'd given when waiting tables. So, despite all the swirling—and unfounded—fears around him that kept other agents up at night, he just kept his head down and went to work, day in, day out.

Now, this isn't to say that Kyrylo was dumb, or unprofessional, or uninformed. It was amazing to watch him work. He was an incredible advocate on behalf of his clients, and he represented them with skill and professionalism.

The key difference was when there were rumors, or worries, or wonderings floating around the office about things that people "heard" or "thought," Kyrylo just didn't care. He never worried about changing interest rates, depressions, market troughs, or housing shortages because, to him, those things were vague, theoretical concepts that didn't really affect the work he did on a day-by-day, person-by-person basis.

If it was important to his client, it was important to him. If not, he simply didn't worry about it, because his mentor never told him he should. He was laser-focused on the things that mattered, and completely ignored the things that didn't.

Years later, and well into his career, when he'd seen and learned enough of markets, and finances and interest rates to understand why they cause concern, he'd already built for himself a business—full of loyal clientele—that could survive any "potential" downturn that "could" happen. So, despite the theoretical, he just kept on doing the practical. Ignoring what *could be*, he just worked on what *was*, and did so with the same foundational skills of customer service he employed when he was happily filling glasses with water and brushing crumbs from tables.

It was as if he wasn't afraid of the boogeyman because no one had told him he should be and he thrived as a result.

Sometimes, not knowing there's something you're supposed to be afraid of is one of the best forms of courage you can have.

Life is full of inherent risks. Nothing is promised. Nothing is guaranteed.

There is, in fact, no such thing as a safe harbor from financial disappointment or economic harm. Literally, even the very heart which beats in your chest at this exact moment isn't guaranteed to offer another pump if it doesn't want to.

Day by day, hour by hour, and minute by minute, we're living by the graces of benevolence, be they from God, karma, or the universe at large. So, if that's true—and I assure you it is—then perhaps we should all just take a deep breath, take a moment to be present, and stop letting the fear of potential shit-storms run amuck in our minds.

Fear affects all members of humanity, but it has a distinct effect on the minds of Real Estate agents.

If you stop and think about it, it makes sense.

When your ability to pay the rent and buy food—your ability to survive—depends on your capacity to close deals, there will always be an aspect of fear that creeps into your consciousness suggesting what *might* happen to us if the deals don't close or the market dries up. The thing about fear is, there's always a "might" or a "could happen" out there to suggest that demise is right around the corner. And technically speaking, there always is a potential for demise.

But, as fear so commonly causes us to forget, there's also an equal potential for success, waiting directly around the very same corner.

I don't care what the market, industry, product, or profession is, there will always be a reason out there to suggest it won't work, or that you shouldn't do it. There's always a reason not to do anything, and if we made a habit of listening to each reason, we'd all probably just sit around in a bunker somewhere waiting to die.

Open up Google, watch YouTube, scroll social media, read the news, or talk to your friends. There will always be someone, somewhere, who's ready to tell you that there's reason to be afraid, that you should stop, panic, and turn in for something safer.

But, the illusion of safety is that it exists, especially in a professional sense.

Sure, a lot of things in the Real Estate game can make us worry or cause us to be afraid. But can you think of a job or an industry out there that is fully secure, or completely sound?

I can't.

In stark contrast to Kyrylo, I've run into many, many other agents who, on paper, seemed like they should have done extremely well in this business.

I've personally witnessed professional marketers with master's degrees, and high-powered economists armed with a thousand spreadsheets, who equally fail while other, seemingly less prepared agents flourish.

Like densely muscled, well-bred racehorses born to race, they broke out of the gate with all the speed and God-given talent in the world. However, after a few laps, and as the race started to get tight, they let their anxieties got the best of them. They started to worry about the other horses, the mud on the track, and the gathering clouds in the sky. Rather than focusing on the ground in front of them, they frantically looked at the horses to their sides, and eventually behind them, wondering if everyone else was worried about the mud, too.

In those moments of mental alarm and inflamed worry, all the muscle, and size, and breeding, and master's degrees in the world couldn't help them despite themselves.

While they got caught up in the muck of the mental moment, the slower, less inherently gifted underdogs—like Kyrylo—focused only on putting one foot in front of the other fast and efficiently, and pulled ahead to the front of the pack.

I can think of several, "purebred" agents I've known whom you would have thought the smart money was on, but who never actually finished the race because they were too busy worrying about what might happen around the next turn.

While most of us may deal with—and be influenced by—fears, worries, anxiety, and the knowledge of uncertainty, the one thing we can do is teach ourselves to *focus on the things that matter, and gradually tune out the things that don't*. And, if in defining what matters and what doesn't, we wonder which course is best, we may eventually find our backs against the wall of professional uncertainty, which dictates faith and trust as the virtues most needed to move forward in search of success.

And despite all the fear, the one thing I implore you to remember is that success is always found on the other side of the failure coin. Keep showing up, keep putting in the work, keep honing your skills, and *keep flipping that coin*.

The beautiful thing about winning is that, despite all the failures, you often only need one winning flip to offset them all.

And it's that one winning flip, after a hundred losses, and despite all the fear, that makes all the difference.

chapter fifteen

THE NEW RULES OF REAL ESTATE

You've reached the final chapter.

Congratulations to you.

By now, you should know how much I hate Real Estate Gurus, and the pervasive effect they have on our entire industry. However, I will put my anti-guru reputation on the line here for just a moment as I share something with you that's slightly guru-esque.

Over my years in Real Estate, I've learned a lot of lessons. These lessons have all been born of personal experience. These are things I've learned, through trial and error, for myself. These lessons, in my mind, are the very principals that allowed me to survive in the Real Estate business when I was 3 months in, thousands of dollars in credit card debt, and behind on my mortgage. It was learning these lessons that, in a very real sense, saved me from having to quit being an agent and head back to Corporate America with my tail between my legs.

I see these "lessons" as so transformative for business success, that, frankly, I've come to call them rules.

These rules, much like a type of equation, have evolved to be a touchstone for me: a set of criteria which, if adhered to, would allow me to succeed despite any personal or market weakness I may face.

And so, despite not wanting to pretend to guru-ness, I offer them to you—a set of rules for success in the modern Real Estate World.

For me, I call them: The New Rules of Real Estate: Principals For Success By Focusing on People.

As for you, you can call them whatever the hell you want.

THE NEW RULES OF REAL ESTATE

1. Put People First, Paychecks Second

2. Adapt to Your Environment

3. Become Obsessed with Understanding Value

4. Realtors Are Luxury Items—Act Like It

5. Be Trustworthy, Not A Salesperson

6. Seek Mentors, Not Gurus

7. Remember Why You're Doing This

8. Trust That You'll Succeed

9. Be Financially Prepared for the Storms

10. Beware of Unspoken Assumptions

11. Don't Let Your Mood Control Your Work

12. Homes Are Emotional Things

13. Don't Suck on Internet Cigarettes

14. Remember The Law of Opportunity

15. Forget to Be Afraid

Without wanting to overstate things, I'll tell you this much: if you not only memorize them, but do your best to honestly internalize them, they'll change your life and business more than anything else I've found.

If you do that, I think you'll find in them the same thing I have:

A genuine concern for the wellbeing of other people, and the weird kind of success that comes from focusing more on others than you do on yourself.

At the end of the day—and at the end of this book—there's one thing I know to be true:

The Real Estate Business is a unique, crazy, wonderful, and terrifying ride that can <u>mess with your emotions</u> as much (or more) than any other profession.

It's a business full of money, markets, and crazy emotional people mixed in the middle. Clients are emotional. Agents are emotional. Homes are emotional. And there's lots of money changing hands. Mix all of that into a bowl and you've got yourself a recipe for some truly stressful situations.

But this is the game we all signed up for, right?

It's the insanity of the industry that's incredibly fun and f'ing frustrating all at the same time, right?

So, with all that being said, my parting advice to you would be to simply enjoy the ride.

Speaking from experience, as terrifying as the ups and downs of Real Estate can be, it sure beats the hell out of sitting in a cubicle all day waiting for the 5 o'clock bell to ring.

The key to finding joy in the Real Estate journey, despite all the insanity, is to focus on the humanity within it.

Focus on people, build relationships, provide value, and just be the best damn human being you know how to be.

If you're asking for my two cents, that's the key to Keeping It *Real*.

Made in the USA
Columbia, SC
19 December 2020